We need to do a better job training
our office staff, who are the face of the
congregation and who set its Jewish tone....
If the synagogue is to be our sacred space,
our fragment of Jerusalem, then every
employee and every volunteer needs to play
a part in advancing its mission.

Rabbi Eric Yoffie, 2005 Biennial Sermon, Houston, TX

■ *Shalom!*

In many Reform congregations, one of the most crucial roles, greeting and responding to callers—Jews and non-Jews, members and strangers—falls to the administration and support staff. The receptionist, administrative assistant, rabbi's secretary and religious school secretary are *de facto* the face of the congregation. No matter what their personal background and knowledge of Reform Judaism, they act as gatekeepers and often determine the perception of a congregation and sometimes even of Judaism itself. Their ability to respond with understanding and to answer or refer questions appropriately is the beginning of effective Outreach and Membership cultivation.

This manual was developed by the Union for Reform Judaism Department of Outreach and Membership and the National Association of Temple Administrators. It is designed for temple administrators, educators, Membership directors, rabbis and Outreach and Membership chairpersons to use for training all those on the front lines who are involved in direct contact with current and potential members, interfaith couples, individuals exploring conversion and their family members. We hope it opens lines of communication and serves as an impetus for the establishment and implementation of internal policies, whether formal or informal, that are clearly understood by all. We want to ensure a warm welcome for all who approach our congregations.

For best results, staff training is essential. While *Beyond Shalom* may simply be given to everyone who answers the telephone or greets visitors in the congregation, we recommend that it be used as part of an interactive training program during a full staff retreat or as part of a series of two or three shorter sessions. To encourage training, we have included two versions of outlines for the administrator—a one-day comprehensive session and a two-session "Lunch and Learn"—which make it easy to prepare training sessions for your staff.

As Rabbi Eric Yoffie declared in his 2005 Biennial sermon, "The synagogue will thrive only when it extends a loving hand to each and every Jewish soul, both synagogue members and members yet-to-be." And as Shammai advises in *Pirkei Avot* (1.15), "Say little and do much, and greet all people with a cheerful smile."

It is our hope that the use of *Beyond Shalom* will give those who are responsible for meeting people at our gates the knowledge and confidence to extend a loving hand and provide a warm welcome.

Kathryn Kahn, Director
Union for Reform Judaism
William and Lottie Daniel Department
of Outreach and Membership

Loree B. Resnik, FTA, President
National Association of Temple
Administrators

BEYOND *Shalom*

Your Synagogue's Office Guide to Connecting with Warmth and Welcome

Executive Editor
Kathryn Kahn, Director
William and Lottie Daniel Department of Outreach and Membership
Union for Reform Judaism

Editor
Leslie Kyla Klieger, Projects Coordinator
William and Lottie Daniel Department of Outreach and Membership
Union for Reform Judaism

Adviser
Loree B. Resnick, Executive Director
Suburban Temple–Kol Ami, Beachwood, OH
FTA, President, National Association of Temple Administrators

■

We would like to extend special thanks to the consummate professionals
who made *Beyond Shalom: Your Synagogue's Office Guide to Connecting
with Warmth and Welcome* possible. Your expertise and wisdom enabled us
to create a guide that will assist our congregations in going "beyond
shalom" into a genuine, deep and warm welcome. It is our hope
that Reform synagogues, their professional staff and their current
and prospective members will reap the fruits of these efforts.

■

Audrey Wilson, Associate Director
Northeast Council, Union for Reform Judaism

Joyce Engel, Executive Director
Temple Israel of New Rochelle, NY

CONTENTS

Appendixes

A NOTE TO THE ADMINISTRATOR

A training session with your staff will give you the opportunity not only to disseminate the information in this book but also to emphasize that the work they do, helping those who reach out to your congregation, is truly a sacred endeavor. They have the unique opportunity to touch and sometimes change the lives of people in your community.

We have provided two options for *Beyond Shalom* training: a one-session comprehensive training session or a two-session plan that can be conducted over lunch as a "Lunch and Learn" for staff. We encourage you to use one of these outlines to create sessions that address the specific needs of your staff and the particular circumstances of your congregation. The outlines can be found in Appendixes B and C on pages 31 and 32.

We have also included text study pieces to begin the training(s) in order to connect the practical aspects of the work we do with words from our tradition. We encourage you to promote discussion among your staff, whether Jewish or not, using the texts and questions we supply, as well as anything you would like to add. This is a wonderful way to frame the holiness of the work they do. Text and questions can be found in Appendixes D and E on pages 33 and 34.

You should plan to use the exercises in this book along with resources produced by the Union for Reform Judaism and materials from your own synagogue in order to tailor the training to the particular needs of your staff. The list in Appendix A on page 30 includes materials that you should plan to hand out at the training session, one copy for each person attending. These are materials with which you want to be sure they are familiar, in regard to both the concepts and how to implement them. You should choose the scenarios that are most relevant to your synagogue or add any you feel are important. While you do not have to role-play all of the scenarios, you should make sure that your staff is familiar with the policies that each addresses and that they know how to handle each phone call with sensitivity and warmth.

You might also find it valuable to schedule a check-in with your staff approximately six months after the completion of the initial *Beyond Shalom* training. This will give them the opportunity to discuss the calls they have been receiving and ask any follow-up questions they might have. It will also give you the chance to cover scenarios you did not address in the first training session(s) or add additional ones that are relevant to your congregation.

In addition, we have included a section to assist you as well as your Membership Committee and chair with your membership integration after an individual or family joins your congregation. You will find an intake interview training outline, interviewer guidelines, a sample intake interview and a sample interview report in Appendixes G, H, I and J on pages 36–43. When an interfaith family joins your synagogue, there are additional Outreach issues of which you should be aware. In Appendix K on pages 44 and 45 you will find a list of issues with which an interviewer should be familiar and recommendations on how to prepare for interviews, and Appendix L on pages 46 and 47 features a checklist to help you determine how welcoming your congregation is to interfaith families.

OPENING THE DOOR

In each congregation, the first person who responds to a caller about an Outreach or Membership issue becomes an ambassador. Whether the caller reaches the one part-time secretary who serves an entire congregation, a rabbi's secretary or a temple administrator, that staff member is the important first contact this person has with your synagogue, and for some people, it is also their first contact with Judaism and Jewish life. All who serve in this way have a sacred duty and a great opportunity to touch lives and affect the future of Judaism.

WHAT IS OUTREACH AND MEMBERSHIP?

As Reform Jews, we are committed to building vibrant, inclusive congregational communities and actively welcoming all who wish to join us. We seek to perform the mitzvot of *ahavat ger* (loving the stranger) and *keruv* (drawing near all who are far).

Reform Jewish Outreach strives to welcome and embrace prospective and new members, interfaith families and individuals considering conversion while creating vibrant opportunities for individuals and families to deepen their personal connection to Judaism and make Jewish choices in their personal lives. Our population is diverse: Jews and non-Jews, young and old, interfaith and Jewish families, Jews-by-choice and those who are considering conversion. Membership efforts do not cease with the recruitment of new members. We strive for active, lifelong membership through the successful integration of new members into our communities and the ongoing engagement of current members. Through Outreach and Membership, we endeavor to create an atmosphere in which all who seek a place in our congregations find a comfortable home and a sacred community.

OFFERING A WARM FIRST WELCOME

When a person has a question about something Jewish, he or she will often look through the telephone book and begin to make phone calls. You could be the person who answers the call. If you think this is an awesome responsibility, you are right. You are representing Judaism to the caller, particularly if the person is not Jewish. Even when the caller is a Jew, the way you respond often leaves a lasting impression about your congregation and organized Judaism.

Whatever the reason for this person's calling, remember: When you are on that call, *be present.* You may be busy, but to the person on the other end, your attention is invaluable. Stop what you are doing and listen. Often a person is seemingly calling for one reason, with a question or a request, but he or she might be telling you something else subtly. For example, someone calls to cancel a reservation because her husband is ill. Don't just cancel it and hang up. Be aware of her needs, what the synagogue can do for her family. Should you refer her to the rabbi? Alert the Caring Committee? Ask if she would like his name added to the *Mi Shebeirach* list? If you listen actively, you will hear a great deal.

■ TELEPHONE PROFESSIONALISM

The following exercises are designed to help you practice extending a warm welcome from the first shalom to the end of the call. They are adapted from "Creating a Welcoming Atmosphere" and are used with the permission of the Jewish Federation of Greater Atlanta.

ANSWERING THE PHONE

A person calling your synagogue gets an immediate impression of the congregation from the manner in which the call is answered. A bored or irritated-sounding "Congregation Bayit" projects the image of a synagogue that really doesn't care a great deal about its members. That's why the right greeting is so critical to getting each call off to a good start.

Imagine how much more professional and friendly it sounds when you put a smile in your voice and cheerfully say something like "Shalom, Congregation Bayit. This is Marcy. How may I help you?"

Follow these steps:

✓ Greet the caller ("Shalom").

✓ Identify the congregation or department ("Congregation Bayit").

✓ Identify yourself ("This is Marcy").

✓ Offer to assist ("How may I help you?").

PUTTING A CALLER ON HOLD

People place a high value on their time, and therefore so should you. Professional communicators follow these simple rules any time they need to put a caller on hold:

✓ Always ask the caller's permission before putting the call on hold, then wait for a response.

✓ Explain how long it may take to get the answer.

✓ Use the HOLD button. It's unprofessional to leave the phone line open while you are trying to solve a problem.

✓ Never leave a call on hold for longer than one minute without returning to the caller.

✓ Thank the caller for holding.

For each situation below, determine what you would say to the caller when you want to put him or her on hold. Your statements should follow the guidelines stated above and demonstrate that you value the caller's time.

1. Outreach Committee Chairperson Susan Seidman is on the phone. She wants to speak to the executive director about an upcoming program. The director is on another call, but Susan insists on waiting.

2. Eric Goldstein is new to the area and wants to speak with Karen Singer, the Membership director, about joining the synagogue. Karen stepped away from her desk for a moment but will return shortly.

THE MESSAGE YOUR ANSWERING SYSTEM SENDS

Think about the automated answering system at your synagogue. It may be a very sophisticated system—one that directs callers to different extensions and offers a variety of options for obtaining information, including an alphabetical listing of employees and board members. Or it may be as simple as a telephone answering machine.

Points to remember when planning your message:
- Begin with a warm welcome. Start with "Shalom" and a smile: The caller will be sure to hear the welcome in your voice.
- Keep the message as brief as possible or offer bypass options if the message is lengthy.
- If possible, have an option that allows the caller to leave a confidential message in the clergy mailbox.
- If you have a staff directory or extension options, offer them early in the message.
- If your synagogue is small and directs callers to volunteers outside the building, be sure to identify the names and positions of those people.
- If at all possible, have separate extensions for program listings and directions to your congregation. If this is not an option, direct the caller to your synagogue's Web site or leave directions on the machine only if there is an option to bypass the message.
- For after-hours calls, be sure to offer a voice mail option rather than asking the caller to call back during business hours.

Rewrite the script for your recorded message(s), including your own voice mail message if you have one. Remember, the script should create a welcoming atmosphere and should be convenient and user-friendly for the caller.

_____

_____

_____

_____

_____

_____

_____

ACCENTUATING THE POSITIVE

To which of the following were you more likely to better respond as a child?
- *"You cannot go to the movies unless you clean your room."*
- *"You may go to the movies after you clean your room."*

Most of us probably responded better to the *positive* message than to the *negative* one. As adults, we still feel the same way. We just do not like having someone say "no" to us. It lowers our self-esteem.

Think about what you say to callers and visitors. When was the last time you found yourself saying something like the following to a caller?
- *"You have to speak to Rabbi Stern about that."*
- *"We don't do that at Congregation Bayit. It's not our policy."*

You could just as easily have said:
- *"That's a matter Rabbi Stern would be happy to address."*
- *"At Congregation Bayit we suggest that you can..."*

How you deliver your message is important. Here are some guidelines for saying things in a positive manner instead of a negative one:

Negative Messages	Positive Messages
I can't	I can
You can't	You can
I'll try to	I will
You need to	Will you
You should have (blaming)	I'll take care of it (solving)

Below are some statements couched in negative language. How could you word them to accentuate the positive?
1. I don't know where the meeting will be held.
2. You need to talk to the cantor about that.
3. You can't use the meeting room on Tuesday.
4. The bookkeeper's only here in the morning. Please call back tomorrow.
5. We don't allow photographers at services.
6. I'll try to get that information for you.

THE ANGRY CALLER

When you are dealing with angry or upset callers, it often helps to understand what has upset them. Often they are angry about a particular situation, not with a person. Unfortunately, it is the person on the phone who becomes the target of their anger.

Here are some tips for handling an irate caller:

✓ Remain calm and unemotional.

✓ Don't take the caller's anger personally.

✓ Apologize without blaming.

✓ Listen patiently. Summarize or paraphrase to show your understanding of the caller's issue.

✓ Empathize to show that you understand the caller's feelings.

✓ Get as many facts as you can.

✓ Accept responsibility.

✓ Offer the caller solutions if you are in a position to carry them out.

✓ Make sure that the call is transferred to the right person.

KNOWING THE HEART OF THE STRANGER: HOW IT FEELS TO CALL A SYNAGOGUE

The caller who is asking questions about Judaism or Jewish life-cycle events may exhibit one or more of the following feelings, among others:

- Nervousness
- Uneasiness
- Fear
- Confusion
- Apprehension
- Guilt

- Embarrassment
- Anger
- Excitement
- Shyness
- Defensiveness
- Curiosity

Activity

Take turns role-playing the following brief scenarios that have been adapted from actual phone calls. In each case, listen to the tone of the conversation and identify the varied emotions the caller might have. Reflect on the two questions below, then answer the additional questions that appear under each scenario.
- In how many different ways can the scenarios be interpreted?
- What would your own feelings be if you were to take this call?

Address the questions that follow to explore further the feelings conveyed by the caller.

A. "Someone told me that if I join your temple, my husband and I won't be able to be buried together in your cemetery because he is Presbyterian. Is that true? Who can I talk to about this? No, I don't want to give my name. Why does Judaism try to drive us all away?"

   1. This caller seems to be exhibiting a number of the emotions listed above. What do you think they are? Do you think she is aware of them? How does her tone make you feel?

   2. Do you know the policy of your congregation regarding burial? If you know that her statement is false, should you be the one to tell her? Do you think you still need to address her last question?

   3. If you do not know the policy, do you know who does? Is there a policy? Whom could you ask? If the rabbi is not available and the caller does not wish to leave her name, who else could address this issue?

B. Frances Isaacs calls and says, "You sent me High Holy Days tickets, but I don't want to join again this year. Should I mail the tickets back?"

   1. How does Frances feel when she is making this call? What may be her reasons for resigning? Does she understand that she is resigning rather than just not "joining again this year"?

   2. If you don't know who Frances is, can you quickly pull her data file and ascertain whether she is elderly, if her last child has just left religious school or anything else that might be pertinent? What other unspoken scenarios may exist within this call? Is Frances homebound? Has her husband just entered a nursing home, thus greatly stretching their finances? Does she now have three children in college?

3. Who should talk to Frances? What should you say to her if you are going to transfer her call?

4. Is it possible that Frances is experiencing financial hardships and doesn't know how to ask for help? Who will be able to determine that? Who will be able to offer her an adjustment to her dues?

No matter what the question is or how the caller is feeling, your response, your willingness to spend time with the caller and the warmth in your voice are all important. Even if your congregation's policy indicates that you are not the one to provide the answer, when you refer a caller to the right person, you may be the key to helping someone in crisis find a welcome in Judaism.

■ MEMBERSHIP AND OUTREACH CALLS

There is a wide spectrum of potential callers. Your caller may be a knowledgeable Jew; a curious Christian; someone who was born to Jewish parents but has not been involved in Judaism for years; a non-Jew married to a Jew or thinking about marrying one; someone wishing to learn more about Judaism, possibly in anticipation of a future conversion; a parent or grandparent exploring the issues of interdating or intermarriage for an adult child. In any event, you are that person's contact with the synagogue and, for some, with Judaism.

Now that you have identified some of the feelings that callers might have, it's time to take the next step: understanding the policies of your own congregation and clergy. Every synagogue has policies, whether they are formally written or informally verbal, about life-cycle events such as marriage, birth, education, *b'nei mitzvah*, conversion, death and membership concerns, like High Holy Days tickets, dues and availability of programming. As a synagogue employee who works directly with members and inquirers, you need to be familiar with the general policies of your congregation. In addition, there are procedural guidelines about who should respond to a given question and what information should be given in particular circumstances. The examples that follow are designed to help you clarify both your synagogue's policies and procedures.

Activity
Here are some key questions about general Membership issues and Outreach concerns that are commonly posed by temple members and unaffiliated callers. As a receptionist, secretary or administrative assistant, you will be the first to respond to these calls. To make these interactions positive for the caller and more comfortable for you, we suggest that you role-play a variety of responses to each scenario. Use the space provided below each scenario to fill in the information that pertains to your congregation and its policies (use additional sheets if necessary). Then keep this sheet close at hand for easy reference. Take time to adapt or expand the scenarios presented so that you can address additional concerns that arise with some frequency in your synagogue.

Note: It is highly recommended that a congregational rabbi(s), cantor(s), educator and temple administrator take part in these sessions so that information on policies and preferences for handling various situations can be shared. It would be valuable to include the Outreach and Membership chairs as well.

GENERAL MEMBERSHIP

High Holy Days Tickets/Prospective Member

Call: "Hello. This is Alan Martin. I need five High Holy Days tickets. Can you send them to me?"

What you need to know: Whether or not your congregation sells tickets to High Holy Days services, a call like this should never receive a simple "yes" or "no" answer. It provides a great opening to make the caller feel welcomed by your congregation and possibly turn the call into a membership recruitment opportunity.
- What information should you get from the caller? Is he new to the community or just in town for a visit? Is he unaffiliated with a synagogue?
- Has he ever visited your synagogue? If not, be sure to offer a warm invitation to upcoming services and programs.

- What is your congregation's policy on tickets for nonmembers?
- Is "It is not our policy" ever a good answer?
- To whom should you refer this call?

Your congregation's suggested responses to questions about High Holy Days tickets or other prospective member calls:

_____

_____

_____

_____

Religious School/*B'nei Mitzvah*

Call: "My name is Bob Schwartz and I'm not a member of your temple. My daughter, Rebecca, just decided that she wants to have a bat mitzvah. I think it's because she went to her cousin's bar mitzvah in New York and now she wants a bat mitzvah. I would like to arrange for her to have one. What do I have to do?"

What you need to know: During your conversation with this caller, keep in mind that requests for *b'nei mitzvah* and religious school enrollment are an opportunity to connect families to your congregation and the Jewish community.
- What is the process for a child to become a bar or bat mitzvah in your congregation?
- Is there a minimum time that the child must be enrolled in religious school before becoming a bar or bat mitzvah?
- Does a family have to belong to the synagogue in order to enroll their child in religious school?
- Who is the best person for the caller to speak to regarding all of the aforementioned issues?

Your congregation's suggested responses regarding *b'nei mitzvah* and religious school:

_____

_____

_____

_____

Congregational Membership and Dues

Call: "I'd like to know how much the dues are at your synagogue."

What you need to know: When it comes to a prospective member, you don't want the first conversation to be simply about money. Think about how you might steer the conversation toward other information.
- Who handles membership recruitment in your congregation?
- Can you put this prospective member in touch with that person immediately? If not, how should you respond to this question?
- Perhaps you can suggest a visit with the rabbi or a meeting with the Membership chair, executive director or Membership director?
- What upcoming programs would be perfect for this person to attend?

Your congregation's suggested responses to questions regarding membership and dues:

_____

_____

_____

_____

Life-Cycle Events for Nonmembers

Call: "Hello. I'm not a temple member, but my father just passed away and I need to find a rabbi to officiate at his funeral. Is your rabbi available?"

What you need to know: The first thing you should do is offer your condolences for the caller's loss.
- What is the rabbi's policy on officiating at life-cycle events for nonmembers?
- If he or she does not officiate in such circumstances, should you answer the question directly or should you refer it to the clergy or Membership director?
- Is this a matter for the rabbi or Membership director?
- Can you refer the caller to someone in the community who does officiate at life-cycle events for nonmembers?

Your congregation's suggested responses to calls about life-cycle events for nonmembers:

_____

_____

_____

_____

20s/30s Young Adult Programming

Call: "Hi. My name is Isabel Harris. I've just moved to town and I am looking for a temple. Do you have programs for people in their 20s?"

What you need to know: Callers in this demographic are looking for a place where they can feel comfortable and welcome even if they are single or do not have children.
- Does your congregation have special programming for young adults? If so, can you tell the caller a bit about what is available? You should be familiar with all of the basic programming options available in your synagogue.
- To whom should you refer the call for more information—the program director or whoever handles the young adult program?
- If your congregation does not have this kind of programming, what else can you offer Isabel as a prospective member? Could she be served by your congregation and directed to the Young Jewish Professionals division of your local Jewish Federation or does the JCC have young adult activities? Would Isabel be better served elsewhere? Can you say that?
- What if Isabel joined with some others and initiated some young adult activities? Would the congregation be open to and supportive of such programming?

Your congregation's suggested responses to calls about 20s/30s programming:

_____

_____

_____

_____

Empty Nesters

Call: "My husband and I are empty nesters now. Are there any special programs or activities for us? We used to have big family holiday celebrations, but now none of our children live here. Where can we go?"

What you need to know: It is important to make people feel that they are valuable members of the synagogue community whether or not they have children. You should be familiar with the program schedule so that you can tell the caller what is available.
- Does your congregation have a special group that provides such programs?
- Does the congregation have a community seder? A Chanukah dinner? A Rosh HaShanah reception or a break fast? Do you pair up people who want to host a seder or Shabbat dinner with people who would like to have a place to go?
- Do you know about programs in the community?
- Are there materials you can send to the caller or a mailing list she can join?
- Are programs advertised on your Web site?

Your congregation's suggested responses to questions about opportunities for empty nesters:

_____

_____

_____

_____

Gay/Lesbian/Bisexual/Transgender/Diversity

Call: "My name is Betsy Stern. My partner, Julie Morgan, and I are looking to join a temple that has other families like ours. We have adopted a beautiful Chinese daughter, Sophia Morgan-Stern, and want to know if there are other families like ours at your synagogue."

What you need to know: Keep in mind that Betsy and her family are looking for a community in which diversity is embraced and in which they can be comfortable.

- Is Betsy concerned only with the fact that there are families that "look like them" or also that the temple might not be welcoming to people with a different family structure from that of most of its members?
- If there are no other GLBT couples in your synagogue, what else about the congregation would appeal to Betsy and make her feel welcome? Are there others who have adopted children?
- Besides the GLBT issue, Betsy is also asking about Jews of color. What kind of diversity can be found in your synagogue? Who can connect her with others in the congregation who might have similar family situations?
- Who else should talk to Betsy?

Your congregation's suggested responses to questions about gay/lesbian/bisexual/transgender/diversity:

_____

_____

_____

_____

Financial Questions

Call: "I want to join your temple, but I already paid the Building Fund fee at Temple Beth Ami. Would I still have to pay a Building Fund fee to your temple?"

What you need to know: Although this person is already interested in membership, you still want to make the conversation about more than just money and welcome the caller warmly into the community.

- What is the policy of your congregation?
- Does it change based on age?
- Who should be the one to explain this policy?

Your congregation's suggested responses to questions regarding financial matters:

_____

_____

_____

_____

OUTREACH

Jewish Education

Call: "I'm not Jewish but my spouse really wants our children to be raised as Jews. Can your synagogue help me?"

What you need to know: Families often think about congregational affiliation when their children become school age. You should read Appendix M on page 48, Revisiting the 1995 Resolution on Religious School Enrollment, and Appendix O on page 54, the CCAR Resolution on Patrilineal Descent.

- What is your temple's policy on enrollment of children from interfaith families in the religious school?
- What programs, such as Tot Shabbat, does your congregation offer that would help make interfaith families who are exploring synagogue membership comfortable?
- To whom should you direct this call?

Your congregation's suggested responses to questions about religious school and family education:

_____

_____

_____

_____

Birth Rituals

Call: "This is Jeff Schwartz. I'm calling from the hospital. My wife, Megan, who is not Jewish, just delivered a baby boy. Do we have to have a *bris* to give our son a Hebrew name? Could we have a naming at the synagogue later? Does it matter if he's being baptized as well?"

What you need to know: The first thing you should do is congratulate the caller on the birth of his child.

- What is your rabbi's and/or congregation's policy regarding birth rituals for unaffiliated Jews? Does this policy change in particular interfaith situations?
- Are there Reform mohalim (medical professionals certified by the Reform Movement to perform ritual circumcisions) in your community who will circumcise sons of Jewish fathers and non-Jewish mothers who will be raised as Jews?
- Learn about the Reform position on patrilineal descent (see Appendix O on page 54), which opens the door to Jewish identity to offspring of intermarriage when one parent, either mother or father, is Jewish. What are the additional requirements?

Your congregation's suggested responses to questions about birth ceremonies:

_____

_____

_____

_____

Ritual Participation for Non-Jewish Family Members

Call: Marvin Newman says, "My son will become a bar mitzvah next August. My wife, Jody, and her parents are not Jewish. What role can they have in the bar mitzvah?"

What you need to know: First, offer a hearty *mazal tov* on the upcoming celebration. Keep in mind that Jewish life-cycle events can be stressful for those in interfaith relationships. It is important that the entire family feels welcome and supported.
- Do you know your synagogue's answer to the caller's question?
- If you do, should you answer him or refer him to someone else? To whom might you refer the call?
- Are you familiar with the synagogue's policies regarding this and other life-cycle rituals that involve interfaith families?

Your congregation's suggested responses to questions regarding ritual participation:

_____

_____

_____

_____

Congregational Membership

Call: "I'm Jewish, but my husband, Tim, isn't. Do you have special dues rates for interfaith families?"

What you need to know: Often callers may be inquiring about membership and dues, but they may also want to know whether or not your congregation welcomes interfaith families.
- How can you make this conversation about more than the money?
- What is the dues policy for interfaith families at your synagogue?
- How can you let the caller know that all families, including interfaith ones, are welcome in your synagogue?
- To whom should you refer this call?

Your congregation's suggested responses to questions about membership:

_____

_____

_____

_____

Conversion

Call: "This is Katie Lee. I'm thinking about converting to Judaism. What does that involve? Can I talk to someone?"

What you need to know: Callers frequently ask about conversion, wanting to know what is involved, how long it takes or how soon they can start. Others are interested in introductory adult education.

- What is the process of conversion for someone who studies with your rabbi?
- What information should you give about conversion and to whom should you refer the caller?
- Does your congregation have an Outreach brochure about conversion that you can send to the caller, such as the Union for Reform Judaism's *Becoming a Jew: Questions About Conversion*? (see Appendix P on page 57)
- Do you know what introductory level classes are offered in your synagogue?

Your congregation's suggested responses to questions about conversion and adult education:

_____

_____

_____

_____

Weddings

Call: "I have a unique problem. I'm Unitarian and I'm marrying a Jewish woman. Will your rabbi perform the ceremony?"

What you need to know: Be sure to offer the caller your congratulations on his or her upcoming marriage. Similar calls may come from a Jewish or non-Jewish bride or groom, a Jewish or non-Jewish parent or even a friend.

- Does your rabbi or cantor officiate at interfaith weddings?
- If so, under what circumstances? If not, does your rabbi wish to speak with the couple directly and/or make referrals to other clergy who do officiate at such weddings?
- Do you understand the synagogue's policy?
- What exactly should you say (and not say)?
- If the rabbi is not available to speak with the caller immediately, what information should you get from the person?
- Should you congratulate the couple and offer to add their names to your Outreach mailing list? Should you send them a copy of the brochure *Intermarried? Reform Judaism Welcomes You*? (see Appendix R on page 63)

Your congregation's suggested responses to questions about marriage officiation:

_____

_____

_____

_____

Death

Call: The wife of a recently bereaved member of your congregation, Sally Hart, is calling from the monument company, where she is selecting a headstone for her late husband, John. She says, "I know John would have wanted a cross on his headstone. Can I have that at our cemetery?"

What you need to know: First, be sure to offer your heartfelt condolences on the loss of Sally's husband.

- What is the synagogue's policy regarding burial of non-Jewish family members in your temple's cemetery?
- Does your rabbi officiate at the funeral of a non-Jewish spouse?
- Should you be the one to explain that, or should you refer her to someone else?
- What other useful information regarding death, burial and mourning policies and practices in your congregation could you offer?

Your congregation's suggested responses regarding death and burial:

_____

_____

_____

_____

GENERAL QUESTIONS ABOUT JUDAISM AND COMMUNITY CONCERNS

When calls come into the synagogue office asking for information or the "Jewish position" on various issues, you will need to know how to respond. If the caller is a congregant, he or she may be referred automatically to the congregational rabbi. If the person is unaffiliated with your synagogue, the rabbi may also want to take the call.

In many instances, the information is easily accessible and you might be expected to respond. What information should you have at your fingertips? Under what circumstances should you refer a caller to the rabbi, cantor, educator, administrator or a particular lay leader?

Activity

The questions that follow have been compiled from many actual phone calls received by Reform congregations. Review the suggested answers that follow and add other questions of your own. Use the blank spaces provided or add extra sheets. Consider the following: How might each of these callers feel? Are you able to respond to their feelings and give the information requested? If not, to whom would you refer each caller?

You will likely receive calls from Jews-by-choice, interfaith families, people exploring Judaism and Jews who are new to your area. Take the time during this session to determine what your community resources are and create a Resource Directory that can be updated as necessary. You might list a college of Jewish studies, local Judaica shops, temple gift shops, kosher butchers, delis or bakeries, supermarkets that sell kosher products and anything else a caller might want to know. Be prepared to tell callers where, in addition to your temple, adult education classes or cultural activities are offered. Your helpful answers and information can make callers feel more comfortable and welcome in a new environment or with a new Jewish experience. Keep close at hand copies of your congregation's adult education and Outreach program pamphlet as well as the Union for Reform Judaism brochures *Becoming a Jew: Questions About Conversion, An Introduction to Sanctuary Etiquette* and *Intermarried? Reform Judaism Welcomes You* (see Appendixes P, Q and R on pages 57, 60 and 63). For those who are attending a Jewish life-cycle event for the first time, you might also want to recommend the Jewish section of the book *How to Be a Perfect Stranger: A Guide to Etiquette in Other People's Religious Ceremonies,* Volume 1, edited by Arthur J. Magida (Jewish Lights Publishing).

Questions/Responses

How do I sign up for classes to become Jewish?
Determine with your rabbi what the response should be. Most likely, your rabbi will want you to refer the caller to him or her rather than just saying, for example, "Call the Union for Reform Judaism." On the other hand, it's wise to have information available on the basic facts—where, when, cost—about your local Introduction to Judaism class and other Outreach programs, such as A Taste of Judaism: Are You Curious? and Stepping Stones to a Jewish Me, as well as educational or discussion programs for interfaith couples.

_____

_____

_____

_____

Where do I go to buy something my husband calls a "your-sight" (*yahrzeit*) candle?
Know the various local stores that sell this item and share that information. But first, offer to explain what a *yahrzeit* candle is and how it's used (see Glossary on page 74). This applies to any ritual object that a caller may inquire about. Remember, if you are not certain of the answer, refer the call to someone else or offer to find out and call him or her back shortly.

_____

_____

_____

_____

Someone told me that Jewish people don't send flowers for funerals. What should I send?
Discuss the appropriateness of making a memorial contribution or sending food to the shivah home. Again, be ready to explain such terms as "shivah." Suggest some local establishments from which the caller can order food.

_____

_____

_____

_____

I'm invited to a bar mitzvah at your temple, and I've never been to a Jewish service. What will I have to do?
Assure the caller that many visitors who are not Jewish attend your services and then explain the customs of your particular congregation. What is the appropriate attire for men and women? Will most people wear *kippot*? Will a visitor be able to follow the service? Is it appropriate to participate? Also, explain what the caller, as a guest, will not have to do. Offer to send him or her *An Introduction to Sanctuary Etiquette* (see Appendix Q on page 60).

_____

_____

_____

_____

Use the remaining space to add questions that you have had problems answering in the past. How should they be answered?

_____

_____

_____

_____

_____

_____

_____

_____

_____

_____

QUESTIONS FOR REFERRAL

The previous exercises have given you some tools to help you handle a range of potential calls with warmth and sensitivity. Still, you should be aware that among the many calls you receive, some will be of a very personal nature. Realize that the person on the other end of the line may be sensitive and may not want to tell you why he or she is calling. In this situation, graciously connect the caller to the person for whom he or she is asking. At other times, a caller might ask a question that requires more of a conversation than a quick answer and would be better addressed by your clergy, staff professionals or lay leaders. Below are some of the potential calls that most likely should be referred to others in the congregation. Fill in the Call Referral Chart featured in Appendix F on page 35 for an easy reference regarding which person should handle what calls. Add relevant topics from your own experience.

- Prospective Member Inquiries
- Religious School Questions
- Clergy Policy on Life-Cycle Events (Marriage, Baby Naming, Funeral, Etc.)
- Synagogue Dues
- Illness
- Interest in Judaism/Conversion
- Clergy Officiation at Interfaith Life-Cycle Events
- Death
- Resignation
- Anger Regarding an Incident
- Change in Marital Status
- Synagogue Security Concerns
- Change in Employment Status

■ COMPLETING *BEYOND SHALOM*

You have now completed *Beyond Shalom* and are ready to help in the Outreach and Membership efforts of your congregation. You have considered many issues, learned about congregational policies and examined the different feelings that people experience when they make first-time contact with a synagogue. Whether or not you are Jewish, you will be representing Judaism and your congregation to whoever calls. As you can see, your role is one of tremendous importance both to the individuals who call and to the congregation whose welcoming atmosphere is in your hands.

The many questions and concerns that have been anticipated in this manual are only a beginning. The more time you spend as a synagogue staff member, the more Outreach and Membership questions and issues you will handle. Remember, "Thank you for calling us. I don't know the answer, but I will put you in touch with someone who does" is often the very best response you can give.

It is expected that you will have further questions and concerns. A list of resources developed by the Union for Reform Judaism Department of Outreach and Membership can be found on page 75. Know that there are many people as well who are eager to help you in this very important work: your clergy, temple administrator, educator and/or president, as well as your congregation's Outreach and Membership Committee chairs, your Union for Reform Judaism regional director of Outreach and Membership, and the Union for Reform Judaism national Outreach and Membership staff. Fill in their names and numbers, as well as other handy contact information, on the next page for easy reference.

IMPORTANT OUTREACH AND MEMBERSHIP CONTACTS

Your Outreach Committee Chair: _____

    Phone: _____ E-mail: _____

Your Membership Committee Chair: _____

    Phone: _____ E-mail: _____

Union for Reform Judaism Regional Director of Outreach and Membership:

_____

    Phone: _____ E-mail: _____

Union for Reform Judaism Regional Office: _____

    Phone: _____ E-mail: _____

Union for Reform Judaism National Department of Outreach and Membership

    Phone: 212.650.4230   E-mail: outreach@urj.org

Additional Useful Numbers:

    Local Reform mohalim: _____

    Introduction to Judaism class (Union for Reform Judaism or other): _____

    Local Jewish bookstore or Judaica shop: _____

    Local Jewish funeral home: _____

    Local Jewish bakery: _____

    Local Jewish deli or butcher: _____

    Local supermarkets with kosher products: _____

    Other: _____

FOR THE TEMPLE ADMINISTRATOR, OUTREACH CHAIRPERSON OR MEMBERSHIP CHAIRPERSON

Ensuring that the initial phone call from a person with a question receives a positive response is only the first step in welcoming a new member into your congregation. In the Appendixes you will find materials that will help administrators, Membership directors, lay Membership and Outreach chairs and committee members plan the next steps.

OPPORTUNITIES AND CHALLENGES OF THE INTAKE INTERVIEW

The intake interview is a fundamental part of the membership process in most Union for Reform Judaism congregations. A well-constructed intake interview is not just an important aspect of membership-recruitment efforts but also a vital part of membership integration and retention because it sets the stage for what we hope will be a lifelong relationship with the congregation. It provides a key opportunity to establish a tone of openness, to learn about the hopes, fears and expectations of the congregants and to convey some of the policies and *minhagim* (customs) of the congregation.

The intake interview can be conducted by staff or by trained volunteers. A complete overview, an interview training outline, sample interview questions and a report memo can be found in Appendixes G, H, I and J on pages 36–43.

OUTREACH ISSUES IN THE INTAKE INTERVIEW: THE ROLE OF THE NON-JEW IN THE SYNAGOGUE

The intake interview is especially critical for interfaith families that may have no prior experience of synagogue life in relation to interfaith issues. It provides an opportunity to address a range of concerns. While some questions should be referred to the rabbi (see the Call Referral Chart in Appendix F on page 35), the interviewer can go over many policies and practices, particularly those that affect an interfaith family. Even more important, the interviewer can provide assurance of welcome by listening closely and responding with understanding, clarity and warmth.

Ideally, policies that affect interfaith families should be distributed in writing along with general congregational policies and should be discussed in the intake interview or during a special session with the rabbi or educator. If this does not happen, new members may eventually confront an unpleasant "surprise" at a time when they are most vulnerable, such as on the occasion of a child's religious school enrollment or bar mitzvah or a death in the family. Other "surprises" may arise if a member who is not Jewish wishes to be considered for a board or committee chair position and is disallowed because of a policy of which he or she is unaware.

Many Reform congregations have explored and set policies regarding the role of the non-Jew in the synagogue. These policies include issues of membership, governance and ritual. The temple administrator needs to know if policies have been created and, if so, where they can be found. Policy may have been approved by the Board of Trustees and could appear in its minutes or in a separate policy book. It may be a part of the constitution and bylaws. Policy may have appeared as a special letter to the congregation, as a feature in the bulletin, in rabbinic messages or sermons or in some other manner. In some congregations this information appears right in the

Membership brochure and/or new member packets as well. In other congregations the policy is not well publicized. The administrator needs to know if this information has been disseminated to current congregants as well as whether it is available to new members.

If the materials have already been presented to prospective members, then the intake interview can be used to clarify policies, answer questions and alleviate concerns. If they have not, then this is a good setting in which to begin discussion of pertinent policies as they apply to a particular family. Areas in which interviewers should be informed and ready to impart information can be found in Appendix K on pages 44 and 45.

The goal of Reform Jewish Outreach—building vibrant, inclusive congregational communities and actively inviting, welcoming and educating all those who wish to join us—appears to be a reasonable one. Do we achieve it? In Appendix L on pages 46 and 47 you will find a checklist that will help you and other synagogue leaders determine just how user-friendly your temple really is for those who are new to your congregation, to Judaism and to Jewish life. Use it with your temple staff, your Outreach Committee or your Board of Trustees to identify areas of strength and enhance your Outreach capacity.

■ APPENDIX A

MATERIALS TO HAND OUT AT *BEYOND SHALOM* TRAINING

Union for Reform Judaism Publications
- *Becoming a Jew: Questions About Conversion* (see Appendix P on pages 57–59)
- *Intermarried: Reform Judaism Welcomes You* (see Appendix R on pages 63–66)
- Biennial Initiative: Lifelong Synagogue Membership (see Appendix S on pages 67–69)

Your Congregational Resources
- Membership packets
- Mailing lists to which callers can subscribe
- Membership application
- Congregational policies on Membership
- Congregational policies on dues and dues relief
- Adult education brochures
- Upcoming program flyers
- Staff and volunteer policies regarding office administration

Photocopies of
- Text Study
- Activities
- Call Referral Chart
- Glossary

APPENDIX B

SUGGESTED TRAINING OUTLINE (One-Day Session)

Please use information in *Beyond Shalom* to help you plan each section.

    I.   Welcome and Introduction

   II.   Text Study/Discussion

  III.   Importance of Synagogue Community
- *What's Missing from Our Congregations?...YOU*
- Biennial Membership Initiative

  IV.   What Is Outreach?

   V.   How It Feels to Call a Congregation/Role-Play Exercise

  VI.   Short Break

 VII.   In Our Congregation (Your Congregational Resources)

VIII.   Questions to Anticipate/Role-Play Exercise

  IX.   General Questions About Judaism and Community Concerns (FAQs)

   X.   Who Handles What? Filling In the Call Referral Chart

  XI.   Thank You for the Sacred Work You Do

 XII.   Congratulations! You've Completed the *Beyond Shalom* Training.

(Hand-Out Resources/Glossary/Bibliography)

■ APPENDIX C

SUGGESTED TRAINING OUTLINE (Two "Lunch and Learn" Sessions)

Please use information in *Beyond Shalom* to help you plan each session.

Session I

    I.   Welcome and Introduction

    II.   Text Study/Discussion

    III.   Importance of Synagogue Community
- *What's Missing from Our Congregations?...YOU*
- Biennial Membership Initiative

    IV.   What Is Outreach?

    V.   How It Feels to Call a Congregation/Role-Play Exercise

    VI.   Thank You for the Sacred Work You Do

Session II

    I.   Text Study/Discussion

    II.   In Our Congregation (Your Congregational Resources)

    III.   Questions to Anticipate/Role-Play Exercise

    IV.   General Questions About Judaism and Community Concerns (FAQs)

    V.   Who Handles What? Filling In the Call Referral Chart

    VI.   Congratulations! You've Completed the *Beyond Shalom* Training.

(Hand-Out Resources/Glossary/Bibliography)

APPENDIX D

TEXT STUDY FOR *BEYOND SHALOM* TRAINING I

Blessing for Torah Study

בָּרוּךְ אַתָּה יי, אֱלֹהֵינוּ מֶלֶךְ הָעוֹלָם, אֲשֶׁר קִדְּשָׁנוּ בְּמִצְוֹתָיו
וְצִוָּנוּ לַעֲסוֹק בְּדִבְרֵי תוֹרָה.

*Baruch Atah Adonai Eloheinu Melech ha-olam, asher kid'shanu b'mitz'votav v'tzivanu
la-asok b'divrei Torah.*

Blessed are You, Eternal our God, Ruler of the universe, who has sanctified us with Your
commandments and commanded us to engage in words of Torah.

Text

Yose ben Yohanan of Jerusalem says: Let your house be open wide.

Pirkei Avot 1:5 (Ethics of Our Ancestors)

Questions for Discussion

1. How can the synagogue be likened to a house? How does this help us to understand the work
   we do here?

2. What does letting your house be open "wide" mean? To whom are we opening it?

3. What can we, as synagogue staff, do to open our house wide?

■ APPENDIX E

TEXT STUDY FOR *BEYOND SHALOM* TRAINING II

Blessing for Torah Study

בָּרוּךְ אַתָּה יי, אֱלֹהֵינוּ מֶלֶךְ הָעוֹלָם, אֲשֶׁר קִדְּשָׁנוּ בְּמִצְוֹתָיו
וְצִוָּנוּ לַעֲסוֹק בְּדִבְרֵי תוֹרָה.

*Baruch Atah Adonai Eloheinu Melech ha-olam, asher kid'shanu b'mitz'votav v'tzivanu
la-asok e'divrei Torah.*

Blessed are You, Eternal our God, Ruler of the universe, who has sanctified us with Your
commandments and commanded us to engage in words of Torah.

Text

Shammai says: Say little and do much. Receive all people with kindness.
Pirkei Avot 1:15 (Ethics of Our Ancestors)

Questions for Discussion

1. During our busy workdays, we can forget that what we do here is truly sacred work. Dealing
   with people can be difficult, and it is easy to lose our patience. How can we take the edict
   "Say little and do much" and apply it to our work in the synagogue?

2. Which people are we to receive with kindness? Be specific.

3. What does "receiving people with kindness" mean for us who work in the synagogue? What
   are some situations you have experienced in which this has or has not happened? How
   would you want to be received?

APPENDIX F

CALL REFERRAL CHART

Call Topic	Refer To	Extension
Prospective Member Inquiries		
Religious School Questions		
Clergy Policy on Life-Cycle Events (Marriage, Baby Naming, Funeral, Etc.)		
Synagogue Dues		
Illness		
Interest in Judaism/Conversion		
Clergy Officiation at Interfaith Life-Cycle Events		
Death		
Resignation		
Anger Regarding an Incident		
Change in Marital Status		
Synagogue Security Concerns		
Change in Employment Status		

APPENDIX G

THE INTAKE INTERVIEW FOR NEW MEMBERS: OVERVIEW AND GUIDELINES FOR INTERVIEWERS

Objective

The goals of the Intake Interview are:

1. To establish a relationship with new members, a one-on-one connection
2. To help them engage in synagogue life through a better understanding of their interests and skills
3. To provide a follow-up mechanism to connect new members with clergy, lay leaders and/or programs and services based on their needs and interests

Interviewers

A core group of interviewers who meet the following criteria should be chosen by the temple clergy, executive director, Membership director and/or lay leaders:

- Strong interpersonal communication skills and experience
- Passion for and commitment to the congregation
- Knowledge about all aspects of the synagogue's programs and policies
- History of reliability with follow-through

Training

Interviewers should receive formal training to clarify their roles and to familiarize them with the open-ended interview and follow-up procedures as well as the instructions on how to find and pass on necessary resources. See the attached outline for the recommended interview training program.

Where

Interviews are conducted by means of personal visits.

When

Interviews should be conducted within the first three months of membership.

Background

Interviewers must be knowledgeable and have information concerning

1. Committees
2. Worship
3. Lifelong Learning Opportunities
4. Bylaws
5. Affiliate Organizations
6. Outreach and Temple Policies for the Role of the Non-Jew in the Synagogue
7. Social Action
8. Communication/Publications
9. Cemetery
10. Religious School
11. Family and Other Programs
12. Synagogue Demographics

So that you are prepared for any questions or issues that arise, consider having the following with you during the interview:

1. Copy of the temple bulletin
2. List/Schedule of adult education program offerings
3. Religious school information
4. Youth group/Youth programs
5. Information about new member programs throughout the year
6. Information about Outreach programs (if applicable)
7. Synagogue policies on the role of the non-Jew in the synagogue
8. Temple calendar
9. List of all temple committees
10. Copies of Outreach brochures (*Intermarried? Reform Judaism Welcomes You*; *When a Family Member Converts: Questions and Answers About Conversion to Judaism*; *Becoming a Jew: Questions About Conversion*), available from the Union for Reform Judaism Department of Outreach and Membership

Follow-Up   On page 43 is a sample report memo for interviewers to attach to the completed interview so that needed action items are clearly communicated and follow-up can be monitored by the Membership chair or another designated individual.

Interviewers will also meet periodically with the temple president, rabbi, administrator and educator, etc., to share information more informally.

Union for Reform Judaism
William and Lottie Daniel Department of Outreach and Membership
www.urj.org/outreach
212.650.4230

UNION FOR REFORM JUDAISM • 37

THE INTAKE INTERVIEW FOR NEW MEMBERS: TRAINING OUTLINE—FACILITATOR GUIDELINES

Note to the Facilitator

The goal of the Intake Interview for New Members is to get to know each person as an individual and to begin establishing a connection between the member and the congregation through a guided dialogue. A critical element in accomplishing this goal is completing the necessary follow-up to further connect the member with specific information, introductions and desired pathways to engagement based on the needs and interests that surface during the welcome interview.

Interviewers should be carefully selected (see the interviewer criteria listed in the Overview and Guidelines for Interviewers on pages 36 and 37) and personally invited to participate in this program. Interviewers should receive formal training clarifying their roles and familiarizing them with the open-ended interview instrument and follow-up procedures, as well as information on how to distribute necessary resources. See the Training Outline, below.

The training session should be an hour and half long. Keep the mood positive and the meeting moving. Use as much humor as possible, and make sure that the interviewers do not take the task so seriously that they scare themselves.

Training Outline

I.   Introduction

A.   Welcome to the Interviewers
Begin the session by thanking the interviewers for taking the time to attend the training session and for being willing to participate in the program. Each congregation will decide who introduces the program and thanks the participants, the rabbi, the synagogue president and the Membership or Outreach chair. All session leaders should underscore the importance of the program and the training session.

B.   Introductions
Ask each person to introduce himself or herself and share his or her favorite activity at the congregation. This should be a quick, one-line statement. The facilitator should go first, modeling the desired response: "I am _____. I loved being at the Purim carnival with my daughter, or_____."

II. Talking About the Congregation

A.   Congregational Connections
In groups of two or three, share the following:
 •   How did you become involved in the congregation?
 •   What is it about the congregation that is most important to your life?
 •   What makes the congregation unique?

B. Large-Group Processing

The whole group comes back together. Ask the participants to share the highlights of their small groups.

III. The Program: Welcome Interviews for New Members

A. Program Overview
Include the following:
- Process
  - Emphasize the goal of the Intake Interview: What are we trying to accomplish?
  - Summarize the benefits of in-person interviews.
  - Address the timing—the importance of conducting them in the first three months of temple membership.
  - Discuss demographics—the attempt to match interviewers with new members at similar life stages and/or with similar interests (if known).
- Intake Interview
  - Review the Overview and Guidelines for Interviewers (see Appendix G); stress the connection-building goal of the interview and the primary qualities that interviewers should possess.
  - Review the interview instrument.
  - Discuss the conversational and relational nature of the Intake Interview.
- Follow-Up
  - Introduce and review the Intake Interview Report Memo (on page 43).
  - Highlight the critical need for timely follow-up.
  - Review the procedures for completion and follow-up.

B. Program Resources
Congregational Familiarity
- Discuss the items listed under Background in the Overview and Guidelines for Interviewers.
- Review items 1–10 on page 37.

IV. Role-Playing a Intake Interview

V. Closing
- To put the training into context, offer a closing text or thought about the importance of building connections, welcoming the stranger or the sacred nature of synagogue community, etc.
- Thank the volunteers for their time and commitment!

Union for Reform Judaism
William and Lottie Daniel Department of Outreach and Membership
www.urj.org/outreach
212.650.4230

UNION FOR REFORM JUDAISM • 39

APPENDIX I

(To be placed on your congregation's letterhead)

THE INTAKE INTERVIEW FOR NEW MEMBERS

Date: _____

Name of Temple: _____

Address: _____

Phone Number: _____

Fax Number: _____

Web Site: _____

Names of Family Members: _____

_____

Please record person(s) spoken with on this line:

Names: _____

Phone Number: _____

INSTRUCTIONS: The goal of the Intake Interview is to get to know the new member(s) (especially their needs, interests and skills) and to begin establishing a relationship between the member(s) and the congregation. Please use the following suggested questions as guidelines for your conversation!

1. How did you come to join our congregation?

    _____

    _____

    _____

    _____

2. Tell me about your family. (children, extended family)

    _____

    _____

    _____

    _____

3. Tell me about yourself. (profession, interests, areas of expertise, talents)

_____

_____

_____

_____

4. What would you like to tell us about your religious background and that of your partner or spouse? (childhood/former affiliations, level of involvement, camps, youth groups, education)

_____

_____

_____

_____

5. Would you like to tell us about other organizations with which you are involved?

_____

_____

_____

_____

6. What do you hope to gain from your temple experience?

_____

_____

_____

_____

7. What information would you like to know about our congregation and its programs? (religious practices, affiliates, programs, education, lifelong learning opportunities, Outreach, social action, other policies)

_____

_____

_____

_____

8. How do you see yourself becoming involved in temple life?

_____

_____

_____

_____

9. What can we do to make your temple experience more fulfilling?

_____

_____

_____

_____

10. Do you have any questions?

_____

_____

_____

_____

Thank you for your time and participation!

INTERVIEWER: PLEASE RETURN THE INTERVIEW AND COMPLETED REPORT MEMO (on the following page) TO (your congregation's designated contact) BY_____. THANK YOU!

Union for Reform Judaism
William and Lottie Daniel Department of Outreach and Membership
www.urj.org/outreach
212.650.4230

■ APPENDIX J

(To be placed on your congregation's letterhead)

INTAKE INTERVIEW REPORT MEMO

Date: _____

To: Membership Chair (or Other Designated Individual)

From: _____
        Intake Interviewer

Re: Report on the Intake Interview with _____
                                            Congregant Name(s)

Attached is the completed document for my Intake Interview with the above congregant(s). The following are the action items that need to be completed as a follow-up to our conversation:

Action Needed   Suggested Responder   Action Completed*

_____

_____

_____

_____

I also have these additional thoughts/reflections:

_____

_____

_____

_____

The Action Completed column should be used by the Membership chair (or designee) for follow-up tracking purposes.

Union for Reform Judaism
William and Lottie Daniel Department of Outreach and Membership
www.urj.org/outreach
212.650.4230

UNION FOR REFORM JUDAISM • 43

APPENDIX K

OUTREACH ISSUES THAT AFFECT PROSPECTIVE AND NEW MEMBERS

For Informational and Intake Interviews

- Ways in which those who are not Jewish can and cannot participate in temple life (as members, in study and worship, on committees and in leadership positions, such as board officers or committee chairs)

- Life-cycle participation for non-Jewish family members

- The way voting is handled in the congregation: whether it is one vote per membership unit or per adult member and whether or not someone who is not Jewish can vote

- Policy on what happens to the non-Jewish partner's membership if the Jewish spouse dies or gets a divorce and whether there is a different policy if there are children in the religious school

- Synagogue policy on dues for interfaith couples: If the congregation has a single dues rate and a married dues rate, whether said rate applies to interfaith couples or whether it is different if both attend the synagogue or if one is church-affiliated. Whether there is a different dues rate offered to all or used only if a special request is made and who makes that decision

- Religious school enrollment policy regarding the education of children from intermarried homes and ways in which all parents can or are expected to take part and who determines this policy: Whether your congregation follows the Union for Reform Judaism-recommended policy (see Appendix N on pages 52 and 53) that children who are also enrolled in formal religious education of another faith may not be educated in the religious school

- Synagogue policy on clergy officiation at interfaith weddings or whether the clergy make their own officiation decisions

- Availability of activities and programs for interfaith couples and their children through Outreach programming of the congregation and what is available to the children who will not be enrolled in congregational religious schools

- Availability of Outreach programs and information about conversion

- Whether non-Jewish members can be buried in the synagogue's cemetery and what arrangements are made for interfaith families

- Resources available in the community for interfaith families (recommended and not recommended)

Steps to Take

- Find out about your synagogue's policies on the role of non-Jews in both governance and ritual areas. Have available copies of the membership brochure, including these policy statements.

- Create a list of synagogue programs that are especially appropriate for interfaith families (Outreach programs, a learners' minyan, Tot Shabbat, etc.) and make it available during your interview.

- Identify interfaith couples who are well-integrated members and who would be willing to speak about their temple experience with prospective interfaith members.

- Gather Outreach resources from the URJ Press (**www.urjpress.com**), such as *Defining the Role of the Non-Jew in the Synagogue* and *The Outreach and Membership Idea Book* series. Use them for guidance in articulating and disseminating your congregation's policies and communicating its commitment to Outreach.

- Work with your educator to coordinate Intake Interviews and registration forms. (Sample registration forms can be found in the two publications mentioned above.)

IS YOUR CONGREGATION USER-FRIENDLY?
AN OUTREACH CHECKLIST

Go through this Outreach Checklist to determine just how welcoming your congregation is toward interfaith families. Check off all that apply to your congregation, and then check your score at the end.

Interfaith Couples

☐ Does your congregation do something special to welcome interfaith couples?

☐ Does your congregation regularly schedule a discussion group for interfaith couples?

☐ Does your congregation offer any kind of programs or workshops specifically designed to integrate interfaith couples/families?

☐ Are there clearly defined ways in which a parent who is not Jewish can participate in the life-cycle ceremonies of his or her child (e.g., bar/bat mitzvah, baby naming)?

☐ Does your congregation have a certified lay Outreach Fellow who works with and programs for interfaith families?

Jews-by-Choice

☐ When your rabbi sponsors someone for conversion, is the new Jew welcomed publicly during a Shabbat service or in some other way?

☐ Does your congregation offer any kind of programs or workshops that are specifically designed to integrate new Jews-by-choice?

☐ Does your congregation have a certified lay Outreach Fellow who is trained to work, under the supervision of your rabbi, with those in the process of conversion?

General Outreach

☐ Does your congregation offer programs that explain the liturgy for Shabbat and other holiday celebrations in a nonthreatening setting?

☐ Are workshops demonstrating the how-tos of Shabbat and festivals offered at your congregation?

☐ Does your congregation offer A Taste of Judaism: Are You Curious?

☐ Is Introduction to Judaism part of your congregation's adult education program? If so, is the course available to nonmembers? If not, is there an Introduction to Judaism class offered locally by the Union for Reform Judaism?

☐ Is there an Outreach section in your congregation's library?

☐ Does your congregation have an active Outreach Committee?

Parents of Interfaith Couples

- ☐ Does your congregation offer programs for congregants whose children have married someone who is not Jewish?

- ☐ Do you provide mentoring workshops for Jewish grandparents whose grandchildren may have a non-Jewish extended family?

Adolescents

- ☐ Do your high school and/or youth groups offer workshops on Jewish identity, interdating, intermarriage or conversion?

Religious School

- ☐ Do your teachers take part in regular in-service training to address interfaith issues that arise in the classroom?

- ☐ Do your teachers send home materials concerning holiday and life-cycle celebrations (e.g., how to make Shabbat at home or how to hold a Passover seder, etc.)?

- ☐ Does your religious school offer parallel programming for parents and children to learn more about Jewish life?

- ☐ Do you provide a First Steps program for children of interfaith families that have not made a decision about the religious identification of their children?

Membership Policies

- ☐ Does your membership application elicit information concerning conversion to Judaism or interfaith marriage? If so, are new members who qualify given information about your Outreach program?

- ☐ Is your policy about membership, governance and ritual roles regarding those partners who are not Jews clearly and sensitively stated in your Membership materials?

- ☐ Does your congregation make provision for burial and mourning of non-Jewish family members?

Count up your check marks. Did you score 18 or above? Congratulations! Your congregation is most welcoming. 12–18? Not bad, but there's room for improvement. 11 or below? Please contact your regional Outreach director to determine the best way to raise your score and make your congregation more warm and welcoming.

APPENDIX M

REVISITING THE 1995 RESOLUTION ON RELIGIOUS SCHOOL ENROLLMENT

Train a child in the direction to take, and when he is old, he will not depart from it.

Proverbs 22:6

The tenth anniversary of the Atlanta resolution on Religious School Enrollment presents an opportunity to revisit the goals of the resolution and how they are reflected in congregational policy and practice today. The Atlanta resolution recommends that our congregations develop clearly articulated and sensitively written religious school enrollment policies. Such policies encourage interfaith families to make informed choices about their child's religious identity. The resolution holds that these policies are in concert with the mission of our religious schools: to work in partnership with parents to educate children in our Jewish tradition, helping them develop strong Jewish identities and spiritual lives that will sustain them. Faith development in the interfaith family can be a complex process. Congregations that implement clear enrollment policies are well positioned to offer support and education to interfaith families, empowering them to raise Jewish children. In Reform congregations across North America, there are many parents, brought up in other religions, who are raising their children as Jews with pride, love and open support.

A couple's choosing Judaism exclusively as their children's religious identity does not preclude a sharing of the non-Jewish partner's religious traditions. In fact, children should not be discouraged from occasionally accompanying non-Jewish parents or grandparents to their worship services or from participating in extended-family holiday celebrations. The non-Jewish parent should be free to share his or her cultural traditions and not be made to feel invisible in his or her child's religious life. Participation in cultural and familial traditions should be distinguished from formal religious instruction.

The Resolution

In 1995 the UAHC adopted a resolution called Enrollment Policies in Reform Religious Schools, which concerned children from interfaith families. The following excerpt encapsulates the main points of the resolution:

> The Reform religious school is a primary pathway for Outreach to interfaith families. As Reform Jews, we welcome interfaith families and encourage them to affirm the Jewish identification of their children. However, experience tells us that some interfaith couples who seek to enroll their children in Reform religious schools are not raising and educating their children exclusively as Jews. This is a path that committed Reform Jews cannot support. First, it is contrary to our understanding of Outreach (which, while deeply respecting other religions, offers a way into Judaism as a distinctive and precious way of life and faith); because it is theologically inconsistent for a person to identify as both Jewish and Christian (or as an adherent of any other religion); because psychologically placing the burden of such an impossible decision on children may imperil their healthy spiritual development; and because it is incongruent with the mission of Reform religious schools, i.e., to teach Judaism as a faith that is lived and to enable students to develop a strong, positive Jewish identity.

THEREFORE, the Union of American Hebrew Congregations resolves to:

1. Establish a clearly articulated policy that offers enrollment in Reform religious schools and day schools only to children who are not receiving formal religious education in any other religion;
2. Develop clear and sensitive procedures for communicating the goals of the school and its enrollment policy to all parents, particularly interfaith parents;
3. Provide and strengthen programs for interfaith couples who are seeking to choose a religious path for their families; and
4. Call on the Outreach and Education Commissions to develop models for policies and programming to open the way for interfaith couples and their children to choose Judaism.

In the ten years following the 1995 Enrollment Policies in Reform Religious Schools, some of our Reform congregations have chosen to adopt the resolution in full, others follow it in practice without written policy and some congregations have no policy or practice about this issue to serve as a guideline for religious school enrollment.

Congregations with Written Policy Statements

- Open Communication   Sensitively written policy statements give prospective members a clear picture of the synagogue they are joining and its expectations.
- Face-to-Face Conversations   In some congregations, educators and clergy inform all parents of the school admission policy in face-to-face meetings. These meetings occur before a family joins the synagogue. This initial personal contact encourages ongoing dialogue.
- Programs for Exploration   With the understanding that faith development is a process, some congregations have created programs designed to introduce children and families to Jewish life. These programs provide a safe way for interfaith families to wade into the waters of Judaism for a short amount of time without external pressure.
- Encourage Informed Choice   Clearly defined expectations coupled with programs that encourage exploration give parents the opportunity to understand more about Judaism before choosing a single faith for their family.
- Trial Periods   Some congregations permit religiously undecided interfaith families to enroll their children in early religious school classes (such as kindergarten, first grade or second grade) for an experimental period. Ideally, at the end of each school year, parents, clergy and educators meet as a team in order to evaluate the events of the year and discuss family faith development. The parents then make an informed decision regarding the future religious education of their family. This can occur before a child enters first, second or third grade.

Congregations without Written Policy Statements

- Unwritten Policies   In a recent survey of congregational educators, the majority of respondents report that their schools have no written policy about a single religious identity for their students. However, the same schools confirm that religious education is reserved for children who are being raised exclusively in the Jewish faith. Even though there is no written policy in many congregational schools, it is clear that an unwritten single-faith policy exists. However, interfaith parents may be completely unaware of this policy.
- Don't Ask, Don't Tell   In the absence of clear communication, a culture of "don't ask, don't tell" may arise. Many respondents report that they articulate their unwritten policy to interfaith families only if they are asked. However, for many reasons, interfaith families often do not inquire about this issue.

  One congregation reports, "We assume that a family bringing children to our synagogue intends for the children to have a Jewish education. Sometimes we don't know if a child has issues relating to this subject until they manifest them in the classroom setting because we do not initiate discussion of the topic." In a "don't ask, don't tell" culture, parents are not free to discuss their educational goals for their children. Telling the truth may have serious consequences to their child's enrollment.

- Enforcement on an Individual, "Case-by-Case" Basis   Unwritten policies are difficult to enforce. In congregations that have unclear policies, rabbis, cantors and educators deal with conflict on an individual basis. The lack of equality in approach may give congregants the perception that certain individuals receive preferential treatment.

The leadership of the Union for Reform Judaism recommends the implementation and communication of enrollment policies in our religious schools. Transparency and openness are vital elements of this process so that interfaith families understand a congregation's policy before they join that synagogue. If a congregation does not have a clearly articulated policy, many interfaith families may enroll in synagogue schools under the assumption that they can raise their child as both Christian and Jewish.

We recommend that congregational leadership revisit the resolution and consider the following recommendations:
1. Congregations should develop and disseminate religious school enrollment policies that endorse the 1995 resolution and are clearly and sensitively written.
2. All new member families who enroll their children in religious school should attend intake interviews with the educator, principal and/or clergy. Enrollment policies should be addressed openly with interfaith parents. Parents should be told the reasons for the policies, the mission of the religious school and the opportunities for support and guidance that are available to help them make a decision about the religion of their child.

Sample Policy Statement
Congregation Emanu-El B'ne Jeshurun of Milwaukee, WI, welcomes all who wish to draw closer to Judaism. To that end, we affirm the position of the CCAR, articulated in 1983, as follows:

> The Central Conference of American Rabbis declares that the child of one Jewish parent is under the presumption of Jewish descent. This presumption of the Jewish status of the offspring of any mixed marriage is to be established through appropriate and timely public and formal acts of identification with the Jewish faith and people. The performance of these mitzvot serves to commit those who participate in them, both parent and child, to Jewish life. Depending on circumstances, mitzvot leading towards a positive and exclusive Jewish identity will include entry into the covenant, acquisition of a Hebrew name, Torah study, bar/bat mitzvah and *Kabbalat Torah* (confirmation). For those beyond childhood claiming Jewish identity, other public acts or declarations may be added or substituted after consultation with their rabbi.

This is the official position of Reform Judaism in America. We recognize the child of an interfaith marriage as fully Jewish provided that the parents have agreed to raise their child as a Jew and are following up on that decision.

In keeping with the resolution of the Union for Reform Judaism, enrollment in our religious school is open to
- Children who are being raised and educated exclusively as Jews, and
- Children who are not concurrently receiving formal education in another religion.

We assume that any child registered in our religious school is being raised exclusively in the Jewish faith and that this is a joint decision and commitment on the part of both parents.

If you are struggling with this decision or uncertain of its implications, we urge you to speak with either the rabbi or the director of Lifelong Learning before registering your child in religious school.

Congregation Emanu-El B'ne Jeshurun, Milwaukee, WI

Resources to Support Your Congregation, Religious School and Educators

Defining the Role of the Non-Jew in the Synagogue: A Resource for Congregations, URJ Press, 2003, Section 9 (p. 210) titled "And You Shall Teach Them Faithfully to Your Children," offers
- Samples of sensitively written model policies from our Reform religious schools
- Examples of religious school intake interviews for parents, including a "Checklist for Educators" (p. 215)
- A model in-service teacher training about Reform Jewish Outreach and issues of interfaith in the classroom titled "Using Your Policy: Getting the Word Out" (p. 174), which has additional written policies about religious school enrollment that affirm and support parents.

To order this publication, visit **www.urjpress.com** or call 212.650.4120.

ENROLLMENT POLICIES IN REFORM CONGREGATIONS

Resolutions Adopted by the Union for Reform Judaism
Enrollment Policies in Reform Religious Schools

Adopted by the General Assembly
November 30–December 3, 1995, Atlanta

Background
The Reform religious school is a primary pathway for Outreach to interfaith families, inviting them into an active Jewish community and giving them the tools to make Jewish choices. As Reform Jews, we welcome interfaith families and encourage them to affirm the Jewish identification of their children through covenant and naming ceremonies, consecration, Torah study in our religious schools, Bar/Bat Mitzvah and confirmation. These are mitzvot that affirm "a positive and exclusive Jewish identity" for a child with one Jewish parent that are enumerated by the CCAR in its declaration on patrilineal descent (1983).

We recognize that enrollment of children in a Jewish religious school is a complex decision that interfaith parents do not undertake lightly. It can have profound implications for the children, the couple and the household they have created and can entail significant sacrifice, particularly for the parent who is not Jewish. We respect the desire and acknowledge the challenge for interfaith parents to impart knowledge and appreciation of the heritage of both parents to their children, while giving them a singular and firm religious foundation on which to grow. Further, we know that such a decision can and often does lead the whole family to a deepened connection with the synagogue at many levels, not only the school. When a family grows and feels enriched by living as Jews, the Jewish community too is blessed.

Admission to Reform religious school of children whose parents have decided to raise and educate them as Jews is fully consistent with the mission of our schools, which, broadly stated, is to teach Judaism as a faith that is lived, and to enable students to develop a strong, positive Jewish identity that is acted on in relation to God, Torah and Israel.

However, experience tells us that some interfaith couples who seek to enroll their children in Reform religious schools are not raising and educating their children exclusively as Jews. They may wish to educate their children in both Judaism and another religion with the idea that at a later time the children will decide which religion is right for them. Or they may choose to identify and educate their children as "both."

This is a path that we as committed Reform Jews cannot support. First, it is contrary to our understanding of Outreach which, while deeply respecting other religions, offers a way into Judaism as a distinctive and precious way of life and faith. Second, it is theologically inconsistent for a person to identify as both Jewish and Christian (or as an adherent of any other religion). Indeed, it is the long-standing policy of the Commission on Reform Jewish Outreach to encourage interfaith couples to choose a single religious identification for their children. Third, psychologically placing the burden of such an impossible decision on children may imperil their healthy spiritual development. Finally, the goal of parents to educate children in both Judaism and another religion is incongruent with the mission of Reform religious schools as articulated above. Without diminishing rights of parents in determining the religious education of their children, our Reform religious schools must nevertheless insist on fulfilling the purpose of making committed adult Jews out of Jewish children.

THEREFORE, the Union of American Hebrew Congregations resolves to:

1. Encourage congregations to take the following steps:
   a. Establish a clearly articulated policy that offers enrollment in Reform religious schools and day schools only to children who are not receiving formal religious education in any other religion;
   b. Develop clear and sensitive procedures for communicating the goals of the school and enrollment policy to all parents, particularly interfaith parents; and
   c. Provide and strengthen programs for interfaith couples who are seeking a religious path for their families, encouraging them to explore Judaism. We call for the expansion of Outreach programming, such as alternative family education programs, holiday celebrations and worship services, Introduction to Judaism classes, Stepping Stones, Taste of Judaism, and interfaith couples' workshops; and

2. Call on the URJ–CCAR Commission on Outreach and Membership together with the URJ–CCAR–NATE Commission on Education to develop and provide models for setting policy and examples of policy, and to encourage congregations to offer appropriate programming to open the way for interfaith couples and their children to choose Judaism.

APPENDIX O

CCAR RESOLUTION ON PATRILINEAL DESCENT

Resolution Adopted by the CCAR
The Status of Children of Mixed Marriages

Following is the final text of the Report of the
Committee on Patrilineal Descent
Adopted on March 15, 1983

The purpose of this document is to establish the Jewish status of the children of mixed marriages in the Reform Jewish community of North America.

One of the most pressing human issues for the North American Jewish community is mixed marriage, with all its attendant implications. For our purpose, mixed marriage is defined as a union between a Jew and a non-Jew. A non-Jew who joins the Jewish people through conversion is recognized as a Jew in every respect. We deal here only with the Jewish identity of children which one parent is Jewish and the other parent is non-Jewish.

This issue arises from the social forces set in motion by the Enlightenment and the Emancipation. They are the roots of our current struggle with mixed marriage. "Social change so drastic and far reaching could not but affect on several levels the psychology of being Jewish…. The result of Emancipation was to make Jewish identity a private commitment rather than a legal status, leaving it a complex mix of destiny and choice" (Robert Seltzer, *Jewish People, Jewish Thought*, p. 544). Since the Napoleonic Assembly of Notables of 1806, the Jewish community has struggled with the tension between modernity and tradition. This tension is now a major challenge, and it is within this specific context that the Reform Movement chooses to respond. Wherever there is ground to do so, our response seeks to establish Jewish identity of the children of mixed marriages.

According to the Halacha, as interpreted by traditional Jews over many centuries, the offspring of a Jewish mother and a non-Jewish father is recognized as a Jew, while the offspring of a non-Jewish mother and a Jewish father is considered a non-Jew. To become a Jew, the child of a non-Jewish mother and a Jewish father must undergo conversion.

As a Reform community, the process of determining an appropriate response has taken us to an examination of the tradition, our own earlier responses, and the most current considerations. In doing so, we seek to be sensitive to the human dimensions of this issue.

Both the Biblical and the Rabbinical traditions take for granted that ordinarily the paternal line is decisive in the tracing of descent within the Jewish people. The Biblical genealogies in Genesis and elsewhere in the Bible attest to this point. In intertribal marriage in ancient Israel, paternal descent was decisive. Numbers 1:2, etc., says: "By their families, by their fathers' houses" (*lemishpechotam leveit avotam*), which for the Rabbis means, "The line [literally: 'family'] of the father is recognized; the line of the mother is not" (*Mishpachat av keruya mishpachah, mishpachat em einah keruya mishpachah, Bava Batra* 109b, *Yevamot* 54b; cf. *Yad, Nachalot* 1.6).

In the Rabbinic tradition, this tradition remains in force. The offspring of a male *Kohen* who marries a Levite or Israelite is considered a *Kohen*, and the child of an Israelite who marries a *Kohenet* is an Israelite. Thus: *yichus*, lineage, regards the male line as absolutely dominant. This ruling is stated succinctly in *Mishnah Kiddushin* 3.12 that when *kiddushin* (marriage) is licit and no transgression (*ein avera*) is involved, the line follows the father. Furthermore, the most important parental responsibility to teach Torah rested with the father (*Kiddushin* 29a; cf. *Shulchan Aruch, Yoreh Deah* 245.1).

When, in the tradition, the marriage was considered not to be licit, the child of that marriage followed the status of the mother (*Mishnah Kiddushin* 3.12, *havalad kemotah*). The decision of our ancestors thus to link the child inseparably to the mother, which makes the child of a Jewish mother Jewish and the child of a non-Jewish mother non-Jewish, regardless of the father, was based upon the fact that the woman with her child had no recourse but to return to her own people. A Jewish woman could not marry a non-Jewish man (cf. *Shulchan Aruch, Even Ha-ezer* 4.19, *lo tafsei kiddushin*). A Jewish man could not marry a non-Jewish woman. The only recourse in Rabbinic law for the woman in either case was to return to her own community and people.

Since Emancipation, Jews have faced the problem of mixed marriage and the status of the offspring of mixed marriage. The Reform Movement responded to the issue. In 1947 the CCAR adopted a proposal made by the Committee on Mixed Marriage and Intermarriage:

> With regard to infants, the declaration of the parents to raise them as Jews shall be deemed sufficient for conversion. This could apply, for example, to adopted children. This decision is in line with the traditional procedure in which, according to the Talmud, the parents bring young children (the Talmud speaks of children earlier than the age of three) to be converted, and the Talmud comments that although an infant cannot give its consent, it is permissible to benefit somebody without his consent (or presence). On the same page the Talmud also speaks of a father bringing his children for conversion, and says that the children will be satisfied with the action of their father. If the parents therefore will make a declaration to the rabbi that it is their intention to raise the child as a Jew, the child may, for the sake of impressive formality, be recorded in the Cradle-Roll of the religious school and thus be considered converted.

> Children of religious school age should likewise not be required to undergo a special ceremony of conversion but should receive instruction as regular students in the school. The ceremony of Confirmation at the end of the school course shall be considered in lieu of a conversion ceremony.

> Children older than Confirmation age should not be converted without their own consent. The Talmudic law likewise gives the child who is converted in infancy by the court the right to reject the conversion when it becomes of religious age. Therefore the child above religious school age, if he or she consents sincerely to conversion, should receive regular instruction for that purpose and be converted in the regular conversion ceremony. (*CCAR Yearbook*, Vol. 57)

This issue was again addressed in the 1961 edition of the *Rabbi's Manual*:

> Jewish law recognizes a person as Jewish if his mother was Jewish, even though the father was not a Jew. One born of such mixed parentage may be admitted to membership in the synagogue and enter into a marital relationship with a Jew, provided he has not been reared in or formally admitted into some other faith. The child of a Jewish father and a non-Jewish mother, according to traditional law, is a Gentile; such a person would have to be formally converted in order to marry a Jew or become a synagogue member.

> Reform Judaism, however, accepts such a child as Jewish without a formal conversion, if he attends a Jewish school and follows a course of studies leading to Confirmation. Such procedure is regarded as sufficient evidence that the parents and the child himself intend that he shall live as a Jew. (*Rabbi's Manual*, p. 112)

We face today an unprecedented situation due to the changed conditions in which decisions concerning the status of the child of a mixed marriage are to be made.

There are tens of thousands of mixed marriages. In a vast majority of these cases the non-Jewish extended family is a functioning part of the child's world, and may be decisive in shaping the life of the child. It can no longer be assumed *a priori*, therefore, that the child of a Jewish mother will be Jewish any more than that the child of a non-Jewish mother will not be.

This leads us to the conclusion that the same requirements must be applied to establish the status of a child of a mixed marriage, regardless of whether the mother or the father is Jewish.

Therefore:
The Central Conference of American Rabbis declares that the child of one Jewish parent is under the presumption of Jewish descent. This presumption of the Jewish status of the offspring of any mixed marriage is to be established through appropriate and timely public and formal acts of identification with the Jewish faith and people. The performance of these mitzvot serves to commit those who participate in them, both parent and child, to Jewish life.

Depending on circumstances, mitzvot[1] leading toward a positive and exclusive Jewish identity will include entry into the covenant, acquisition of a Hebrew name, Torah study, Bar/Bat Mitzvah, and *Kabbalat Torah* (Confirmation).[2] For those beyond childhood claiming Jewish identity, other public acts or declarations may be added or substituted after consultation with their rabbi.

Notes
1. According to the age or setting, parents should consult a rabbi to determine the specific mitzvot that are necessary.
2. A full description of these and other mitzvot can be found in *Sharrei Mitzvah*.

This resolution may be found at **www.ccarnet.org/reso**.

■ APPENDIX P

BECOMING A JEW: QUESTIONS ABOUT CONVERSION
(Department of Outreach and Membership Brochure)

Each year in North America, thousands of people convert to Judaism. While each person's path into Jewish life is unique, there are many shared questions. This pamphlet answers some of these basic questions and suggests additional resources.

1. **Why do people consider converting to Judaism?**
    There are many reasons. Often an interreligious marriage sparks an interest in the non-Jewish partner that can lead to a desire to share the religion of his or her spouse. Similarly, when an interfaith couple decides to raise children, the non-Jew may initially decide to explore Judaism in order to seek a religious common ground for the family. Other men and women seeking religious meaning in their lives, with or without any connection to a Jewish mate, find that Judaism offers them the best medium of religious expression.

2. **Do Jews seek converts?**
    Centuries ago, Jews did engage in proselytizing, particularly during the Graeco-Roman period of Jewish history, when thousands of non-Jews living in Asia Minor embraced Judaism. The destruction of the Roman Empire and mortal threats against Jews who sought converts marked the end of such efforts to gain converts.
    Judaism respects the religious beliefs of others, as well as the convictions of those who choose no religion. At the same time, Judaism is an open religion that readily accepts and encourages those who look to it for fulfillment and guidance in meeting life's challenges. In recent years, the Reform Movement, through its Commission on Reform Jewish Outreach, has taken a more active approach to seeking out people who might choose to become Jews.

3. **How do I know if Judaism is right for me?**
    The best way is to learn as much as you can about Judaism and begin to practice those aspects of Judaism that most appeal to you. Seek out Jewish friends, Jewish family members or a synagogue community for support. As you study and try out Jewish practice and customs at your own pace, you will become comfortable with them and prepare for further steps.
    An excellent way to get a sense of the traditions and practice of Judaism is to take an Introduction to Judaism course. The Reform Movement sponsors these courses throughout North America. You may call a Reform congregation or the regional office nearest you for more information.

4. **If I take an Introduction to Judaism class, will I be expected to convert?**
    No. These courses are offered to anyone who wants to learn more about Judaism. They are most often attended by individuals considering conversion, by interfaith couples learning together about Judaism and making decisions about whether to have a Jewish home, as well as by born Jews who want to learn more about their own heritage. Although many people do take the course as part of their process of choosing Judaism, there are no assumptions or expectations held about people taking the class.

5. **If I decide that I want to become a Jew, how would I go about it?**

    First, make an appointment with a rabbi. The rabbi will not only discuss the process and implications of becoming a Jew but will also explore with you your reasons for wanting to do so. In earlier generations, rabbis would discourage potential Jews-by-choice, turning them away three times to test how serious they were. This custom is seldom followed today, but most rabbis still endeavor to impress upon the potential convert the seriousness of such a choice.

    People considering conversion are expected to study Jewish theology, rituals, history, culture and customs and to begin incorporating Jewish practice into their lives. The scope of the course of study will vary from rabbi to rabbi and community to community. Most now require a course in basic Judaism and individual study with a rabbi, as well as attendance at services and participation in home practice and synagogue life. In order to complete your conversion, there are certain traditional rituals that many Reform rabbis require. Speak to your sponsoring rabbi about what to expect and the meaning of these rituals.

    Keep in mind that you are free to choose the rabbi with whom you will work. Talk to more than one rabbi and find one with whom you are comfortable. This rabbi will then become your guide every step of the way through your conversion. One way to find a rabbi is to call the Reform Outreach director in your area.

6. **If I become a Jew, would people refer to me as a "convert"? Is there some other, more proper term to use?**

    In Judaism, people who become Jews have no less than full Jewish status in every circumstance. For this reason, there may be some objection to any distinctive term that refers to a person who has chosen to become a Jew. On the other hand, many people are proud to let others know they are converts to Judaism. Also, as the number of people becoming Jews continues to increase and as various Jewish religious institutions develop programs to encourage and assist people in this process, it has become useful to talk more publicly about choosing Judaism. Consequently, a number of terms have come into common usage, including "convert" and "Jew-by-choice," often used interchangeably. In our free society in North America today, however, Jewish commitment is a matter of choice for all who are Jews, by birth or conversion.

7. **If I become a Jew, what would be the attitude of other Jews toward me?**

    Judaism has always welcomed those who voluntarily become Jews and considers them full-fledged members of the Jewish community. The Hebrew Bible, as well as later Jewish texts, includes examples of such individuals. The most famous and honored example appears in the biblical Book of Ruth, where Ruth joins the Jewish people and eventually becomes the great-great-grandmother of King David, from whose descendants, according to Jewish tradition, the Messiah will come.

    In our day, most Jews welcome wholeheartedly those who have chosen to become Jews. Nonetheless, some Jews-by-choice report occasional offensive comments directed toward them. Although the reasons for such attitudes are complicated, they are based on ignorance and prejudice and are by no means sanctioned by Judaism. As more and more Jews-by-choice enter the Jewish community, as Outreach and Membership promotes education about Jewish views of conversion and sensitivity to Jews-by-choice, and as public discussion of such a choice grows more commonplace, these negative views will continue to fade.

8. **If I convert with a Reform rabbi, will all rabbis consider me a Jew?**

   Reform, Reconstructionist and, under certain circumstances, Conservative rabbis recognize the validity of conversions performed by rabbis of all branches of Judaism. Many Orthodox rabbis, however, do not recognize non-Orthodox conversions. Your sponsoring rabbi will be able to discuss further any implications for you of conversion under his or her auspices.

9. **If I become a Jew, will I be expected to separate from my family of origin?**

   By no means. Most Jews-by-choice maintain warm relationships with their family of origin. Conversion to a new religion does not suddenly make you over into something altogether new; nor does it cut you off from old family ties or memories.

   However, some converts to Judaism find that, especially initially, their family may be hurt or confused by their choice. Such feelings often result from misunderstandings or a lack of knowledge about Judaism and are, therefore, perfectly understandable. If it happens with your family, what will help immensely is your patience, as well as a willingness to discuss your choice and to show your family that you've not abandoned them.

10. **If I decide not to become a Jew but I have a partner who is Jewish, can our children be raised as Jews?**

    Yes. Many interfaith couples have decided to raise their children as Jews. In many families today, non-Jewish parents play a key role in providing for their children's Jewish education, as well as creating a supportive Jewish home environment. The more you learn about Judaism, the easier this will be for you. Many Jews see such parents as the givers of a precious gift and as a blessing to the Jewish people.

11. **If I decide not to become a Jew, would I be welcome to worship in a synagogue with my Jewish family?**

    Most Reform and Reconstructionist and some Conservative and Orthodox congregations warmly welcome interfaith families to participate in various ways in synagogue life. In following the famous verse from the Book of Isaiah 56:7, "For My house shall be called a house of prayer for all peoples," almost all Jewish religious services are open to the public, so you and your family would be welcome to attend. Sabbath services are held on Friday evening and Saturday morning. Call the specific congregation during the week to find out the times.

12. **If I'm not yet ready to convert to Judaism or if I decide not to, what options do my Jewish partner and I have for our wedding ceremony?**

    This is a very sensitive issue, on which there is a broad range of opinions. We encourage you to seek out a rabbi with whom you feel comfortable and have a thorough discussion about the options.

    No matter what kind of wedding ceremony you have, Reform Judaism considers itself a portal to Jewish life for intermarried families. Through organized Outreach programming and a general atmosphere of openness, an interfaith couple will find a welcome at Reform congregations.

13. **Where can I get more information about Judaism and the process of becoming a Jew?**

    For the names of Reform rabbis in your area and for more information on Reform Judaism, contact the regional director in the area closest to you.

To order this publication, e-mail outreach@urj.org.

APPENDIX Q

AN INTRODUCTION TO SANCTUARY ETIQUETTE
(Department of Outreach and Membership Brochure)

In Your abundant loving-kindness, O God, let me enter Your house,
reverently to worship in Your holy temple.

(Gates of Prayer)

How lovely are your tents, O Jacob, Your dwelling places, O Israel!

(Numbers 24:5)

In order to make your first visit to a synagogue more enjoyable, we are providing the following information, which we hope you will find helpful.

Q. When are Shabbat (Sabbath) services held?

A. In Reform congregations, Shabbat services are customarily held on Friday night and Saturday morning. Check with your local congregation by using the phone book or the Union for Reform Judaism Directory online at **http://data.urj.org/conglist/** to see when Shabbat services begin. Service times may vary, depending upon the community and the occasion. Also, in some smaller congregations, Shabbat morning services are held only if there is a bar or bat mitzvah, so check that, too. You might ask the congregation you call if it is possible to add your name to the temple bulletin mailing list, which usually includes a schedule of all the services.

Q. How will I be greeted and how should I greet those I meet before and after services?

A. When you enter the sanctuary, you may be welcomed with one of the traditional Sabbath greetings, either *Shabbat shalom*, which means "a peaceful Sabbath," or Good *Shabbes*, which means "a good Sabbath." It is appropriate to respond with either of these phrases.

Q. Do I need a prayer book?

A. All synagogues provide worshipers with a prayer book (siddur) on Shabbat. Some congregations offer worshipers a prayer book when they enter the sanctuary; others have prayer books in the bookracks at the seats. There are several prayer books that the congregation may use. *Gates of Prayer* has been the standard Reform prayer book, but some congregations create their own prayer book. In addition, the *Chumash*, which contains the first five books of the Bible with commentary, is used by the congregants to follow the Torah and haftarah readings during the Saturday morning service. Note that the congregation reads together all the italicized print in *Gates of Prayer*. Soon a new prayer book, the *Mishkan T'filah*, will be used by some congregations. This prayer book will have a new format and the content of the Shabbat service will be determined by the congregational leaders of each synagogue.

Q. Should I wear a *kippah*? Should I wear a *tallit*?

A. The tradition regarding the wearing of a *kippah* (yarmulke) and *tallit* (prayer shawl), while varying widely within the Reform Movement, applies equally to men and women. In most congregations, wearing a *kippah* is optional, and *kippot* are provided at the entrance of the sanctuary. If it is the synagogue's custom for worshipers to wear a *tallit*, *tallitot* will also be provided. It is important to note that a *tallit* is worn only during the Shabbat morning service. In some congregations, those who recite the *aliyah* (blessings before and after the reading of the Torah) are expected to wear a *tallit*.

Q. Will I be expected to participate in the service? How will I know what to do?

A. The rabbi or whoever is leading the service will announce the page that you should be on and indicate when you are to stand and sit. You should follow that person's lead and stand and sit with the congregation. Read the prayers aloud and sing at your own comfort level.

During Shabbat services, congregants may be called to the bimah (pulpit) to assist in the service either by blessing the Shabbat candles and wine (only on Friday night), opening and closing the ark or reciting the *aliyah* (blessings before and after the Torah reading). Do not be concerned that you might suddenly be invited to the bimah without warning. All of these honors are usually prearranged, and those who will have them are notified in advance.

During the Saturday morning service, often before and/or after the reading of the Torah, there is a procession around the sanctuary with the Torah scroll. At that time, you may see congregants reaching out and touching the Torah scroll with either their prayer book or the corner of their prayer shawl as the Torah passes. This is a custom that conveys reverence for the Torah, although no one is obliged to participate in it.

Q. When may I enter or exit the sanctuary?

A. Every congregation has its own etiquette, which you can learn by observing or asking questions. However, in almost all synagogues, it is customary to avoid entering and exiting the sanctuary while the Torah is being read. As a courtesy to others, you may decide to remain seated and should avoid going into and leaving the sanctuary when the rabbi is giving the sermon or *d'var Torah*. Because our most reverential times occur when we are standing, you are not to exit or enter the sanctuary at such times.

Q. What should I do with my cell phone and pager?

A. To honor the sanctity of Shabbat and show respect for the service and their fellow congregants, all worshipers must turn off their cell phones and pagers before entering the sanctuary.

Q. What happens after the service?

A. At the conclusion of Shabbat worship, refreshments are usually served. On Friday evening, this gathering is called an *Oneg Shabbat*, which literally means "the Joy of the Sabbath." On Saturday morning, it is called a *Kiddush*, which is also the term for the blessing over the Sabbath wine, because at the *Kiddush*, it is customary to begin by blessing the Sabbath wine and the challah. Everyone is welcome to attend both the *Oneg* and the *Kiddush*.

Q. What is the raised area in the sanctuary called? What ritual objects should I be aware of?

A. The raised area either in the center or on one side of the sanctuary where services are conducted is called the bimah. Behind the center of the bimah, facing the congregation, is the *Aron HaKodesh* or holy ark, which houses the Torah scrolls. In the front of the ark hangs the *ner tamid* or eternal light, which burns constantly as a reminder of God's Eternal Presence.

Q. What is a guideline for accepted dress at Shabbat services?

A. We honor the separateness and sanctity of Shabbat by wearing appropriate attire. Customarily, business attire, such as a suit, dress, nice slacks or a skirt and a shirt or sweater, is suitable wear for Shabbat services. Check with the congregational rabbi if you have any questions regarding the proper dress for Shabbat.

If there is anything else that concerns you either before you attend Shabbat worship or afterward, please do not hesitate to speak to the rabbi of the congregation at which you picked up this brochure.

Do not separate yourself from the community.

(Pirkei Avot 2:5)

Developed by the New Jersey–West Hudson Valley Council
Union for Reform Judaism
William and Lottie Daniel Department of Outreach and Membership

■ APPENDIX R

INTERMARRIED? REFORM JUDAISM WELCOMES YOU
(Department of Outreach and Membership Brochure)

Yours, mine, ours: Every couple begins with two individuals from different backgrounds. Interfaith couples and their families also face the special challenges posed by different religious traditions and sometimes cultures. For more than twenty-five years, Reform Judaism has made a commitment to couples with one Jewish partner to welcome them as a couple within our community, to embrace them and their children, and to offer support and education for their extended families.

Each interfaith love story is unique, but many of them share common themes and concerns. This pamphlet answers some basic questions and suggests additional resources.

Q. I am Jewish; my partner is not. Are we welcome as a couple to attend worship services in the Jewish community?

A. Yes! The prophet Isaiah said: "My house shall be called a house of prayer for all peoples" (Isaiah 56:7). We know from the Torah that from the very earliest days, there have been individuals who lived with the Jewish community but who were not themselves Jewish. Contact your local synagogue to find out about times for Sabbath worship on Friday nights and Saturday mornings, as well as for information about holiday services. For help in finding a synagogue in your neighborhood, visit our Web site at **http://data.urj.org/conglist/**.

Q. I am not Jewish. Are there parts of the service reserved only for Jews?

A. You are welcome at all regular services in the synagogue and, of course, at any life-cycle events to which you are invited (for example, a wedding). Each congregation has its own specifications regarding who may lead services and perform certain roles, but you are welcome to participate in everything that is done or read by the whole congregation at a service. If you have questions or concerns, please feel free to ask the clergy or lay leaders.

Q. I don't read Hebrew. How can I possibly follow the service?

A. Most Reform congregations in North America use both English and Hebrew in the service and provide English translations for many of the Hebrew prayers and readings. If you wish to participate in reading the Hebrew aloud, transliterations for common prayers in the service are often available. (A transliteration is a phonetically written version of a prayer.) Transliterations usually appear in the back of Reform prayer books, and you can also ask if other transliterations of prayers are available. It is perfectly acceptable to read only the parts of the service with which you feel comfortable or to just sit and listen. If you need help finding the place in the prayer book, simply ask someone nearby. Temple members want visitors to feel welcome and at ease during services.

Q. What is the best way to learn more about Judaism? I don't want to take a "conversion" class.

A. Introduction to Judaism and other basic Judaism courses are offered by Reform congregations in many communities. The classes cover such topics as Jewish ideas about God, Torah and other Jewish texts, how to celebrate the holidays, and Jewish life-cycle events. A practice Passover seder or a Shabbat event is often featured. Such classes provide you with an opportunity to pose your own questions about Jewish life, belief, and practice.

While some of those who take Introduction to Judaism classes may be considering conversion, many take them for other reasons. The classes can be particularly helpful to those who are not Jewish themselves but are considering raising a Jewish child and to those who wish to be more comfortable at Jewish family events, such as a Passover seder. For further information about Introduction to Judaism classes, contact your local congregation or your regional office. Classes in major cities can be located on the Web at **www.urj.org/outreach**.

Many congregations also offer Outreach programming to help members and newcomers (both Jews and non-Jews) learn more about the Jewish way of life.

Q. Do I have to be Jewish to belong to the temple? Do I have to be Jewish to serve on a committee or on the Board?

A. Every congregation has its own rules about membership, participation, and governance. There is no central authority that dictates these matters. Most congregations include interfaith couples as members and will welcome your participation on committees and in other facets of congregational life. Ask the clergy or lay leaders any questions you have about membership, or call the temple office and request to be directed to the proper person.

Q. Will I be pressured to convert if we join a synagogue?

A. The Jewish community takes delight in welcoming those who choose to embrace Judaism as their own religion. Our Sages, however, have made it very clear that a conversion is not valid if it results from any pressure or coercion. You are welcome in Reform synagogues as a friend of the Jewish people. You do not have to convert.

Q. As an interfaith couple, we wonder what choices we have about our wedding.

A. Some rabbis will officiate at a wedding between a Jew and a non-Jew under certain circumstances; others will not. Most Reform rabbis, whether or not they choose to officiate, are eager to meet with you to discuss your individual situation. The issues involved are complex. We encourage you to find a rabbi with whom you feel comfortable and discuss all your options at length.

Whatever choice you make about your wedding, past or future, you are welcome in Reform synagogues. Reform Judaism is committed to providing an atmosphere of welcome in congregations as well as specific programming that embraces and supports interfaith couples as they make and live out their Jewish choices.

Q. If a Jew marries a non-Jew, what are the children?

A. Traditional Jewish law says that membership in the Jewish people is matrilineal, that is, passed through the mother. Therefore, matrilineal descent means that if the mother is a Jew, the children are automatically Jewish, too; but if the father is the Jewish parent, the children are not Jewish regardless of the practice in the family home. However, in 1983, after much study and discussion, the Central Conference of American Rabbis, the rabbinic body of the Reform Movement, ruled that children with one Jewish parent (mother or father) will be recognized as Jews if they are raised and educated exclusively as Jews. For Reform Judaism, Jewish identity for children is a matter of parental decision.

For more information about patrilineal descent and how it affects your family, we encourage you to contact a Reform rabbi.

Q. So if religious identity involves making a choice, how do we choose? Who should make the decision?

A. Children depend on their parents to teach them about identity in many areas of life. Interfaith couples must make this decision for themselves and their children. It is our experience that children who are given roots in one tradition are more likely to feel a secure sense of belonging. Children who are raised in both traditions too often feel that they do not truly belong in either community. This is a highly personal decision for parents to make and should be approached with respect for both traditions. Often couples find it helpful to contend with these issues in the context of an interfaith couples group. For referral to such a program, contact a rabbi or your regional office.

Many interfaith couples have chosen to raise their children as Jews, and the Reform Movement welcomes them and their children. In those families, non-Jewish parents often play a key role in providing for their children's Jewish education and in creating a Jewish home environment. If you have decided to raise your children as Jews, contact your local congregation as early as possible to find out what support programs and which people are available to assist you in learning about Judaism and raising your Jewish children.

Q. We are considering enrolling our child in a religious school. Are parents who are not Jews welcome to participate in religious school classrooms and events?

A. Jewish tradition puts a high value on family life. We encourage both parents to be involved in their child's religious school experience, and we welcome your participation. Many congregations offer Outreach and other adult education programming that will help you take part fully and comfortably in your child's religious education.

Q. What about the non-Jewish grandparents? Can they be part of my Jewish child's life?

A. Yes! A child who knows his or her grandparents is a fortunate child. All grandparents are welcome to attend services and events at the synagogue and your child's religious school. Shabbat dinner on Friday nights constitutes a special time for family gatherings that can include grandparents. Grandparents can share family stories, customs, and jokes. A child's relationship with a grandparent is a treasure and should be nurtured.

Q. I have questions that do not appear in this brochure. How can I learn more?

A. For the names of Reform rabbis in your area and for more information about Reform Judaism, contact your regional office. For more general information about Judaism and to learn more about interfaith relationships, the following books are excellent resources:

- Cowan, Paul, with Cowan, Rachel. *Mixed Blessings: Overcoming the Stumbling Blocks in an Interfaith Marriage.* Penguin Books, Inc., 1988.
- Diamont, Anita, with Kushner, Karen. *How to Be a Jewish Parent.* Schocken Books, 2000.
- Einstein, Stephen J., and Kukoff, Lydia. *Every Person's Guide to Judaism.* URJ Press, 1989.
- Friedland, Ronnie, and Case, Edmund, eds. *The Guide to Jewish Interfaith Family Life: An Interfaith Family.com Handbook.* Jewish Lights Publishing, 2001.
- Glaser, Gabrielle. *Strangers to the Tribe.* Houghton Mifflin Co., 1997.
- Kean, Jim. *Inside Intermarriage: A Christian Partner's Perspective on Raising a Jewish Family.* URJ Press, 2006.
- Kertzer, Rabbi Morris N. *What Is a Jew?* Macmillan Publishing Co., 1993.
- King, Andrea. *If I'm Jewish and You're Christian, What Are the Kids?* URJ Press, 1993.
- Levin, Sunie. *Mingled Roots: A Guide for Grandparents of Interfaith Children.* URJ Press, 2003.

Many good resources are available on the Internet.
- The Union for Reform Judaism Department of Outreach and Membership at **www.urj.org/outreach**.
- **www.interfaithfamily.com**, a Webzine and community calendar for programs for interfaith couples.

APPENDIX S

BIENNIAL INITIATIVE: LIFELONG SYNAGOGUE MEMBERSHIP

The synagogue is the heartland of the Jewish world. It is the foundation of our communal existence and the center of our collective life. It is the place where we make room for God and the Jewish spirit. It is where Jews find comfort and refuge from the insecurities of their existence. It is the home where Jews build community, reinforce the bonds of the Jewish family, and keep alive the three things on which our existence depends: Torah (Jewish study), *avodah* (Jewish worship) and *g'milut chasadim* (acts of loving-kindness).

Rabbi Yoffie's Biennial Challenge
Reform Judaism Magazine, Summer 2005

OUTREACH & MEMBERSHIP

Strengthening Outreach and Membership in Reform Congregation

Lifelong Synagogue Membership and Your Congregation

What can we do to help ensure that the covenant between our synagogue community and its members is lasting and sacred?

Membership, the lifeblood of your congregation, is best nurtured when the individuals in your community are known, valued and supported throughout their individual and family life cycle. The information and resources that follow will assist your synagogue to become a place where lifelong membership is an important part of the culture and values of your community.

How Does My Congregation Begin?

Welcoming and involving new members and engaging and retaining longtime members will require the attention and commitment not only of your Board of Trustees and Membership Committee but also of every member of your congregation. Listed below are program offerings that create connections among members, lead to meaningful relationships and give your lay leaders opportunities to create a community where affiliation becomes a sacred covenant between member and congregation.

Getting Started

The following resources can be found on your Biennial Initiative CD and on the *new* Outreach and Membership Web site.

- *A Two-Year Action Plan for Your Congregation's Membership Committee to Attract, Engage and Foster Lifelong Members*
  This resource will help you to create an individual action plan that begins with small steps and continues with more advanced suggestions to assist your congregation in attracting, engaging and fostering lifelong membership.
- *Reaching Out and Reaching In: Re-envisioning Membership in Your Congregation*
  This booklet will help your congregation's Board of Trustees and Membership Committee refocus on the structure, mission and purpose of this important committee and its ability to improve all aspects of the membership process.

- **Coordinate Membership Interviews for Every New Member**
  The new-member interview is an opportunity for congregants to learn about incoming members and for these new members to meet one-on-one with a member of the synagogue. This resource includes a sample interview script and an orientation session for the volunteers who will be meeting with your new members.
- **Establish an Ambassador Program That Matches New Members with Longtime Members**
  This two-year program will ensure that all new members will make connections with existing members and clergy by encouraging their involvement and connection with congregational ambassadors.
- **Make Yearly Phone Calls to Your Entire Membership**
  When members of the Board of Trustees connect personally with members of the congregation for no other reason than to extend a warm holiday greeting and to find out "how things are going," they send a strong message of caring and concern.
  This membership phone survey will assist your leadership in communicating with your entire membership through yearly phone calls.

Leadership Training Opportunity

- **Membership Fellows Certification Program**
  Join community builders, Membership chairs and committee members, temple presidents, administrators, board members and other lay leaders for an intensive four-day program. Study with leading congregational rabbis and experienced program staff of the Union for Reform Judaism, and discover how to open the doors to your congregation wider than ever before with membership strategies and "best practices."
  In addition, participants will assess the strengths and weaknesses of their home congregation in the areas of advertising, synagogue Web sites, new member intake and programming for retention. All participants will gain community-building skills to create a membership structure that recognizes and attends to the three distinct components of lifelong membership: recruitment, integration and retention.
  For more information and to download an application, visit **www.urj.org/membership**.

Membership Publications For Your Congregation

- **New!** *The Life Cycle of Synagogue Membership* **(revised and expanded 2005)**
  Calling all presidents, administrators and Membership chairs! Make this publication a part of your temple library today!
  This newly revised and expanded resource helps congregations more effectively welcome and integrate new members and retain members throughout the life cycle of membership. This resource includes diagnostic exercises for congregational Board of Trustees and Membership Committees and offers programmatic suggestions and congregational best practices that include mission statements, assessment scales, membership ads and forms, new member interviews and much more. This important new publication will show your congregation effective ways to attract the unaffiliated, integrate those who have recently joined and maintain connections to those who call your congregation "home." Bonus: This publication includes an interactive CD full of membership essentials that can be adapted for your own congregation.

- **New!** *The Outreach and Membership Idea Book*
  This cutting-edge collection of *brand-new*, Belin Award-winning programs contains offerings from Reform synagogues all over North America. This resource is the seventh volume of the *Idea Book* series and is filled with successful, creative and innovative programs that are sure to begin or revitalize successful Outreach and Membership offerings in your synagogue for interfaith couples, new and lifelong members, 20s/30s, Jews-by-choice and born Jews who are seeking a community and knowledge of our tradition.

Both publications are available from the URJ Press at **www.urjpress.org** or by phone at 888.489.8242.

Union for Reform Judaism
William and Lottie Daniel Department of Outreach and Membership
www.urj.org/outreach/membership
212.650.4230

APPENDIX T

BIENNIAL INITIATIVE:
INVITING AND SUPPORTING CONVERSION

I make this covenant and its sanctions not with you alone, but both with those who are standing here this day before *Adonai* our God and with those who are not yet standing with us here this day.

Deuteronomy 29:13–14

What Do We Mean by Inviting Conversion?

Asking someone you care about to consider conversion is simply an *invitation*. It means that you value the individual and wish to share a tradition that you consider precious. Inviting conversion is a loving proposal that is offered when a relationship has been established either between two individuals or between an individual and our Jewish community. Coercion or pressure of any sort should never be present in this dialogue.

Conversion involves a solemn covenant whereby one party makes a commitment to Judaism and the other party (individual or community) makes a commitment of acceptance and support.

> The Torah was given in public, openly, in a free place. Had it been given in the Land of Israel, the Israelites could have said to the nations of the world. "You have no share in it." But since it was given in the wilderness, in a place free for all, everyone wishing to accept it could come and do so.
>
> *M'chilta*

Why Should We Extend an Invitation?

In our Reform congregations, there is no doubt that those who have converted bring a special passion and dedication to their Judaism and to our community. Seventy-five percent of converts affiliate with a synagogue compared with fifty-five percent of born Jews. Those who convert have a high level of Jewish education and congregational leadership involvement and often inspire their Jewish partners to immerse themselves more deeply in Judaism. Clearly, we as a community benefit tremendously from the affiliation of Jews-by-choice; therefore, we need to make sure that the path to Judaism is clearly marked and that interested individuals feel encouraged and empowered to begin this Jewish journey. Often those who have been a part of our community for years tell us that they never considered conversion because they didn't know how to begin or because "No one ever asked me!"

> In the absence of Outreach, there would be far fewer Jews-by-choice. Yes, Judaism speaks the language of fate, but it speaks as well the language of choice. We extend an open invitation to those to whom our tradition speaks: Join us.
>
> Rabbi Eric Yoffie

Who Can Extend the Invitation?

There are two ways in which to invite someone to consider becoming a Jew. One is a verbal invitation. This can and should be extended by a loving partner, friend or clergyperson and occurs almost always in the context of a personal relationship.

The second way to invite or encourage conversion is without words—a nonverbal invitation. This happens when a congregation has a culture of supporting, recognizing and honoring those who convert to Judaism. Congregations that view conversion as a public *simchah* for the individual and the community, that offer an opportunity for converts to speak to the congregation about their journey and that educate their members about conversion as an adult life-cycle event invite conversion every day without saying a word. This kind of invitation is extended by and is the responsibility of everyone in our congregations. Our lay leadership can build a congregational culture that encourages and empowers all of its members to become Jews "by choice."

Let's Get Started!

Here are two resources that will help your congregation begin. You will find them on your Biennial Initiative CD and on the Outreach and Membership Web site at **www.urj.org/outreach**.

- *A Two-Year Action Plan for Your Congregation to Recognize and Honor Non-Jews Raising Jewish Children and to Invite and Support Conversion*
  This is a comprehensive two-year plan for your congregation to help it develop a culture of welcome and invitation for those who are interested in exploring conversion.

- *18 Ways to Invite and Support Conversion in Your Congregation*
  Want to create a culture of invitation and support for Jews-by-choice in your synagogue? Here are eighteen effective ways to begin and to continue.

On the Twentieth Anniversary of Outreach
Rabbi Eric Yoffie

Maimonides says that if you love God, then you will want to share that feeling with others. Our obligation as Reform Jews and as servants of God is to reach out to… all those on the margins and to communicate to them the power and the beauty of our Jewish heritage.

Still, our synagogues emphasize the beauty and grandeur of the ancient and awe-inspiring faith known as Judaism, and we joyfully extend membership in our covenantal community to all who are prepared to accept the responsibilities that it entails.

Special sensitivities are certainly required. We can ask but should not pressure. We can encourage but should not insist.

Most non-Jews who are part of synagogue life expect that we will ask them to convert…and they are more than a little perplexed when we fail to do so. It is important to handle the invitation with sensitivity.

APPENDIX U

BIENNIAL INITIATIVE:
SUPPORTING INTERFAITH FAMILIES—
RECOGNIZING AND HONORING THE NON-JEWISH SPOUSE

When a stranger resides in your land, you shall not wrong him. The stranger who resides with you shall be to you as one of your citizens; you shall love him as yourself, for you were strangers in the land of Egypt:

I am *Adonai* your God.

Leviticus 19:33–4

Why Should My Congregation Be a Part of This Initiative?

Parents who are not Jewish but are welcome members of our congregations are often lovingly and supportively raising their children as Jews. In many congregations they are the unsung heroes of our modern Jewish communities, volunteering their time, supporting our synagogues and learning about our tradition so they can teach their children in turn. They give us the priceless gift of future Jewish generations. What kind of support and education does your congregation offer them? How do your lay leaders, clergy and religious school teachers ensure that these parents have the tools to create a Jewish home? And just as important, how does your congregation honor and recognize their dedication to raising children in a tradition that is not their own?

> I'm not Jewish. How will it be possible for me to help raise Jewish children actively without converting or feeling diminished? How will I be able to raise my child in a tradition and religion I wasn't raised in without feeling like an outsider?
>
> Maureen Goldberg

How Can We Begin?

Educating your members to understand and address the often difficult issues that are faced by the non-Jewish parent is the first step to supporting and encouraging Jewish choices for the interfaith families in your synagogue. Listen to their voices; find ways to let them know how important they are in the life of your congregation; empower them to celebrate Judaism in their home; offer meaningful ways in which they can participate in the life-cycle celebrations of their children.

Let's Get Started!

Here are two resources that will help your congregation begin. You will find them on your Biennial Initiative CD and on the Outreach and Membership Web site at **www.urj.org/ outreach**.

- *A Two-Year Action Plan for Your Congregation to Recognize and Honor Non-Jews Raising Jewish Children and to Invite and Support Conversion*
  This is a comprehensive two-year plan to help your congregation develop a culture of recognition of and support for the interfaith couple raising Jewish children.

- *18+ Ways to Welcome and Support Interfaith Families in Your Synagogue*
  Want to create a culture that embraces, supports and encourages Jewish choices for interfaith families in your synagogue? Here are 18+ ways that will help your congregation begin and continue.

Leadership Training

- **The Outreach Fellows Program for Interfaith Family Certification**
  Visit our Outreach and Membership Web site at **www.urj.org/outreach** to read and download the brochure and application.

Want to empower interfaith couples in your congregation to make Jewish choices in their lives? Give your synagogue the gift of an Outreach Fellow, who will be certified to program and lead groups for interfaith couples and families. Join us and learn from Union for Reform Judaism and HUC–JIR staff by exploring the issues of interfaith couples and learn how to implement successful, cutting-edge programming for both interfaith couples and born Jews who are seeking knowledge of our tradition in your congregation.

The Blessing of the *Gerei Toshav*

Excerpted from an article by Rabbi David B. Cohen
Congregation Sinai, Milwaukee, WI

Even in biblical times, Jews met and fell in love with non-Jews. Take Moses, for example, who married Tzipporah, the daughter of a Midianite priest. Even then, the non-Jews who dwelled among us—referred to biblically as *gerei toshav*, or resident aliens—were the support and help that made Jewish existence possible.

Have things really changed? Consider: How often is the non-Jewish partner the one who maintains the rhythms of the Jewish home? Whether lighting candles for Shabbat or a holiday, wrapping Chanukah packages, preparing *charoset* for a seder, planning the details of a baby naming or bat mitzvah or driving in the carpool—it is often the non-Jewish partner in the proverbial driver's seat.

That so many choose to contribute to Jewish continuity is astounding and a blessing we ought not take for granted. Even more, the *gerei toshav* in our midst sometimes do so at great personal sacrifice.

It is clear that the *gerei toshav* in our congregation and other Reform congregations everywhere have added immeasurably by their presence and participation. Every Jewish family, every Jewish child, is precious. To those *gerei toshav* who have made this possible, we owe the highest debt of gratitude. Let's not take this blessing for granted. Let's make sure the *gerei toshav* in our midst feel as welcome as they should.

GLOSSARY

For a more complete glossary of terms, visit the Outreach and Membership Web site at **www.urj.org/outreach**.

Aliyah—Literally, "going up." The honor of being called to recite the blessings over the Torah during a service.

Bar mitzvah (m.)/Bat (bas) mitzvah (f.) (*b'nei mitzvah*, pl.)—The ceremony that marks a youngster's reaching the age of religious majority.

Bris (*Brit Milah*)—Literally, "covenant of circumcision." Traditionally performed on the eighth day of a boy's life.

Kippah (*kippot*, pl.)—A head covering worn for religious purposes. Also called a yarmulke.

Kosher home—Literally, "ritually fit." A home that conforms to the Jewish dietary laws.

Minhag—Custom.

Minyan—A prayer quorum of ten adults.

Mohel/Mohelet (mohalim, pl.)—An individual who performs ritual circumcisions.

Seder—Literally, "order." The ceremonial meal that begins the observance of Passover.

Shabbat—Sabbath.

Shivah—The seven-day mourning period that begins with the burial.

Yahrzeit candle—A special candle that is lit in the home on the anniversary of the death of a close relative. It is also lit on Yom Kippur.

Yarmulke—Yiddish word for *kippah*.

UNION FOR REFORM JUDAISM OUTREACH AND MEMBERSHIP RESOURCES FOR YOUR CONGREGATION

Brochures

- *Becoming a Jew: Questions About Conversion*
  This brochure answers basic questions about conversion in an easily accessible question-and-answer format.

- *Honoring Diversity, Seeking Inclusion and Building a Community of Common Purpose*

- *Intermarried? Reform Judaism Welcomes You*
  This brochure answers some basic questions and suggests some additional resources.

- *Introduction to Sanctuary Etiquette*
  This brochure can also be copied and personalized for use in individual congregations.

- *Inviting Someone You Love to Become a Jew*
  It's not always easy to talk about conversion with someone you care about deeply. This material will offer some sensitive and respectful ways to begin the conversation.

- *Leadership Development for Your Synagogue Leaders*
  Trained facilitators who work directly with Boards of Trustees and congregations on membership recruitment, integration and retention are available to consult with your congregation.

- *Primer on Print Advertising: Reaching Beyond Synagogue Walls*
  This primer was designed to help your congregation effectively advertise your temple's entry programs in the secular print media so that you can welcome those who are already looking for you.

- *Reaching Out and Reaching In: Re-envisioning Membership in Your Synagogue*

- *Welcoming and Engaging 20s and 30s: What Can Your Congregation Do?*
  This brochure helps you engage 20s and 30s in activities in your congregation.

- *What Judaism Offers for You: A Reform Perspective*
  For those who desire a brief glimpse into the wonders of Judaism—born Jews, Jews-by-choice, interfaith couples and their families, the wide diversity of seekers—this article gives a brief introduction to Judaism, its belief, its covenant and its traditions from a Reform perspective.

- *What's Missing from Our Congregation?... YOU!*
  Created to examine the value of belonging to a synagogue as well as to dispel myths about synagogue membership and focusing on the synagogue as a house of worship, a house of assembly and a house of learning, this brochure has been designed to be copied and individualized by your synagogue.

- *When a Family Member Converts: Questions and Answers About Conversion to Judaism*
  As a parent, sibling or close friend, you may be wondering how to react to a loved one's decision to become a Jew. This resource addresses some of those questions.

Flyers

- *18 Ways to Invite and Support Conversion in Your Congregation*
  Here are 18 little suggestions to invite and support conversion in your Jewish community.

- *18+ Ways to Welcome and Support Interfaith Families in Your Synagogue*
  Want to create a culture that embraces, supports and encourages Jewish choice for interfaith families in your synagogue? Here are 18+ ways, from easy to advanced, that your congregation can begin and continue.

- *A Two-Year Action Plan for Your Congregation to Recognize and Honor Non-Jews Raising Jewish Children and to Invite and Support Conversion*

- *A Two-Year Action Plan for Your Congregation's Membership Committee to Attract, Engage and Foster Lifelong Members*

Department Publications

- *Focus on Jewish Diversity* Discussion Guide
  The face of Judaism in North America isn't "changing"; it has changed. This discussion guide is a great tool for facilitating discussion on diversity issues in your synagogue. It can be used at Board meetings, WRJ or Brotherhood study sessions, Membership/Outreach Committee meetings, *Oneg Shabbat* programs, adult education classes or *Shabbatonim*.

- *Invitation to Form a Sacred Partnership: A Covenant of Members*

- *Outreach Families in the Sacred Common: Congregational Responses to Interfaith Issues—* Brandeis Study

  This study was conducted to understand how interfaith families function as members of Reform congregations and how congregations welcome them.

- *Sample Programs for 20s/30s and Your Congregation*

- *A Taste of Judaism: Are You Curious?* Program Guide
  This guide offers program essentials and sample curriculums for starting A Taste of Judaism at your congregation.

Department Checklists

- *18 Ways to Make Gay, Lesbian, Bisexual, and Transgender Members Feel Welcome in Your Congregation*

- *Putting Out the Welcome Mat: A Checklist*
  This questionnaire has been devised to assist your Board of Trustees, your Membership and Outreach Committees or your Housing Committee to evaluate how welcoming your congregation really is.

- *What Is Your Congregation's Membership IQ?*

URJ Press Publications for Outreach and Membership Leadership

- *Defining the Role of the Non-Jew in the Synagogue: A Resource for Congregations* (Revised Edition)
  This revised and updated edition draws on the experience and expertise of the past ten years to guide congregations in a deliberative and successful policy-setting process.

- *Engaging Generation Aleph: A Resource for Young Adults in the Synagogue*
  This is a resource guide for congregations that wish to reach out to unaffiliated Jews in their twenties and thirties.

- *First Steps: A Manual for Introductory Education Programs for Interfaith Families*
  Designed to help synagogues develop successful entry-level programming for interfaith families, *First Steps* contains a variety of program models that can be easily adapted to your synagogue or community. The program designs included here attend to the spiritual and social needs of interfaith families, offering sound advice to congregations seeking to welcome new members.

- *The Life Cycle of Synagogue Membership*
  This newly revised and expanded edition helps congregations more effectively reach out to the unaffiliated, welcome and integrate new members and retain members throughout the life cycle of membership. It is available through the URJ Press at **www.urjpress.com** or by phone at 888.489.8242.

- *The Outreach and Membership Idea Book*
  The all-new *Outreach and Membership Idea Book* features nineteen award-winning programs from synagogues across North America. Learn how these congregations have succeeded in recruiting, integrating and retaining members and in reaching out to the unaffiliated and intermarried, and apply the lessons to your own synagogue.

- *Outreach Programs for New Families: In the Beginning...Having a Jewish Baby and Jewish Parenting Made Simple*
  These are two cutting-edge gateway programs with liberal Jewish content designed to pique the interest of expectant and new parents who wish to understand Jewish rituals and traditions that will help them welcome and introduce their new child to Jewish life.

- *The 2004 Outreach Idea Book*
  Stop reinventing the wheel! Ensure successful Outreach programming just by turning a page! *The 2004 Idea Book* is a cutting-edge collection of twenty brand-new, Belin Award-winning Outreach programs selected from Reform synagogues all over North America. This resource is the sixth of the Idea Book series and is filled with successful, creative and innovative programs that are sure to begin or revitalize Outreach and Membership offerings in your synagogue for interfaith couples, 20s/30s, Jews-by-choice and born Jews seeking knowledge of our traditions.

- *The 2002 Outreach Idea Book*
  Continuing in the tradition of previous Idea Books, *The 2002 Idea Book* features the finest and most cutting-edge examples of *keruv* (drawing near those who are far) programming that take place in North American Reform congregations. This book is a must-have for all synagogues looking to improve upon their Outreach and interfaith programming.

- *Working with Interfaith Couples: A Guide for Facilitators*
  A complete guide for those who are organizing and facilitating programs for interfaith couples.

URJ Press Books of Interest

- *Choosing Judaism* by Lydia Kukoff
  This book offers a fresh perspective on the issues that face converts every day: dealing with your non-Jewish and Jewish family, creating your own Jewish community and looking toward the future in your new Jewish faith.

- *Every Person's Guide to Judaism* by Stephen J. Einstein and Lydia Kukoff
  This is a straightforward introduction to Judaism, its customs, ceremonies, theology and practices. Chapters include the Sabbath, festivals, life-cycle events, aspects of faith and the Jewish home.

- *If I'm Jewish and You're Christian, What Are the Kids?* by Andrea King
  In this book, early childhood expert Andrea King tracks the development of two composite families through the life-cycle process and compares how well they manage the challenges that arise at each stage.

- *Inside Intermarriage: A Christian Partner's Perspective on Raising a Jewish Family* by Jim Keen
  Using a healthy dose of humor and insights gleaned from his own experience, Jim Keen provides couples with practical advice and solutions for how to give children a clear Jewish identity while maintaining a comfort level for both parents. This book includes perspectives from professionals who work with interfaith families.

- *Introduction to Judaism: A Course Outline*, compiled and edited by Stephen J. Einstein and Lydia Kukoff
  Since 1983, this has been the standard teaching tool for beginning Introduction to Judaism classes in Reform synagogues and institutions throughout North America. This revised edition has been updated and expanded to include new material in each chapter. Articles, essays, liturgical writings and text sources reflect recent developments in the political situation in Israel, the creation of alternative liturgies and life-cycle celebrations and the Reform Movement's growing emphasis on sacred text and spirituality.

- *Mingled Roots: A Guide for Grandparents of Interfaith Children* by Sunie Levin
  This thoughtful, sensitive book is for every Jewish grandparent who is trying to create a meaningful relationship with his or her interfaith grandchildren.

■ ORDER FORM FOR OUTREACH AND MEMBERSHIP RESOURCES

Fax this form to 212.650.4229 or e-mail outreach@urj.org with your order. An invoice will be included with the order.

To see samples and descriptions of these publications, go to **www.urj.org/outreach/resources**.

(C) = Conversion   (I) = Interfaith   (M) = Membership   (T) = 20s/30s

Quantity _____   *Becoming a Jew: Questions About Conversion* (brochure; no charge) **(C)**

Quantity _____   *Biennial Initiative: Inviting and Supporting Conversion* (booklet; $5 for 10) **(C)**

Quantity _____   *Biennial Initiative: Lifelong Synagogue Membership* (booklet; $5 for 10) **(M)**

Quantity _____   *Biennial Initiative: Supporting Interfaith Families: Recognizing and Honoring the Non-Jewish Spouse* (booklet; $5 for 10) **(I)**

Quantity _____   *18 Ways to Invite and Support Conversion in Your Congregation* (flyer; $3 for 20) **(C)**

Quantity _____   *18+ Ways to Welcome and Support Interfaith Families in Your Synagogue* (flyer; $3 for 20) **(I) (M)**

Quantity _____   *Honoring Diversity, Seeking Inclusion and Building a Community of Purpose* (brochure; $5 for 20) **(M)**

Quantity _____   *Intermarried? Reform Judaism Welcomes You* (brochure; $5 for 20) **(I)**

Quantity _____   *Introduction to Sanctuary Etiquette* (brochure; no charge*)* **(M)**

Quantity _____   *Inviting Someone You Love to Become a Jew* (brochure; $5 for 20) **(C) (I)**

Quantity _____   *Outreach and Membership Recommended Books and Web Resources* (flyer; $3 for 20)

Quantity _____   *Primer on Print Advertising: Reaching Beyond Synagogue Walls* (booklet; $5 for 10) **(M)**

Quantity _____   *Reaching Out and Reaching In: Re-envisioning Membership In Your Synagogue* (booklet; $5 for 10) **(M)**

Quantity _____   *Revisiting the 1995 Resolution on Religious School Enrollment* (booklet; $1 each) **(I)**

Quantity _____   *A Two-Year Action Plan for Your Congregation to Recognize and Honor Non-Jews Raising Jewish Children and to Invite and Support Conversion* (flyer; $3 for 20) **(C) (I)**

Quantity _____   *A Two-Year Action Plan for Your Congregation's Membership Committee to Attract, Engage and Foster Lifelong Members* (flyer; $3 for 20) **(M)**

Quantity _____   *Welcoming and Engaging 20s and 30s: What Can Your Congregation Do?* (brochure; $5 for 20) **(T)**

Quantity _____   *What's Missing from Our Congregation?...YOU!* (brochure; $5 for 20) **(M***)***

Quantity _____   *When a Family Member Converts: Questions and Answers About Conversion to Judaism* (brochure; $5 for 20) **(C)**

Congregation: _____

Street Address (no P.O. boxes): _____

City, State, Zip: _____

ATTN:_____

National Association of Temple Administrators (NATA)

Executive Committee

President	Loree B. Resnik, FTA
Vice Presidents	Susie Amster, FTA
	Janice Rosenblatt, FTA
	Livia Thompson, FTA
Secretary	Nancy Schneider
Treasurer	Edward Alpert, FTA
Past President	Gary S. Cohn, FTA

Board Members

Steven Bram	Jeanne Kort, FTA
Debbie Coutant	Hilary Leboff
Joyce Engel	Carolyn Shane
Suzanne Geshekter	Gary Simms, FTA
Betti Greenstein	Leslie Sporn
Esther Herst, FTA	Marc Swatez, FTA
Jeffrey Herzog, FTA	Sandy Voit
Robert Isaacs	

Union for Reform Judaism–CCAR Commission on Outreach and Membership

Judith Berg, *Chairperson*
Rabbi Stephen Einstein, *Cochairperson*
Austin Beutel, *Vice Chairperson*
Rabbi Howard Jaffe, *Vice Chairperson*

Kathryn Kahn, *Director*
Naomi Gewirtz, *Assistant Director*
Leslie Klieger, *Projects Coordinator*
Emily Wulwick, *Administrative Assistant*

David Aaronson
Marcia Abraham,
 Honorary Life Member
Wendy Adamson
Rabbi Tom Alpert
Susan Ardell
Rabbi Aryeh Azriel
Rabbi Larry Bach
Jim Ball
Rabbi Morris Barzilai
Judy Berg
Rabbi Marc Berkson
Austin Beutel
Rabbi Aaron Bisno
Lisa Bock
Rabbi Eric Bram
Steve Bram
Rabbi John Bush
Paul Cohen
Rabbi Harry Danziger
Georgia DeYoung
Rabbi Michael Dolgin
Rabbi Stephen Einstein
Joyce Engel
Catherine Fischer
Rabbi Steven Foster,
 Honorary Life Member

Cantor Jennifer Frost
Nancy Gennet
Shirley Gordon
Seth Gordon-Lipkin
Barbara Gould
Dorothy Greenbaum
Marcia Grossfeld
Mike Grunebaum
Janice Gutfreund
Rabbi Debra Hachen
Rabbi Stephen Hart
Bob Heller, *Ex Officio*
Diana Herman
Rabbi Howard Jaffe
Rabbi Jerry Kane
Renee Karp
Rene Katersky
Phoebe Kerness
Rabbi Elliott Kleinman
Rabbi Michael Latz
Rabbi Judy Lewis
Carol Lieberman
Rabbi Alan Litwak
Rabbi Jill Maderer
Rabbi Rosalin Mandelberg
Mel Merians,
 Honorary Life Member

Rabbi Jonathan Miller
Paula Milsten
Rabbi Jeremy Morrison
David Oney
Myra Ostroff,
 Honorary Life Member
Rabbi Jack Paskoff
Robert (Mike) Rankin
Rabbi Larry Raphael
Joyce Raskin
Jane Rips
Jon Rosen
Ginny Rosenberg
Marcia Rosenblum
Rabbi Mark Schiftan
Rhea Schindler,
 Honorary Life Member
Rabbi Susan Shankeman
Rabbi Jonathan Singer
Debra Siroka
Rabbi Cy Stanway
Nancy Wiener
Audrey Wilson
Diane Winer
Rabbi Eric Yoffie, *Ex Officio*
Jane Young

UNION FOR REFORM JUDAISM
REGIONAL OUTREACH AND MEMBERSHIP DIRECTORY

Union for Reform Judaism
633 Third Avenue, New York, NY 10017
212.650.4230   Fax: 212.650.4229
Toll free: 1.888.888.6697   E-mail: outreach@urj.org
http://urj.org/outreach/aboutus/staff/

REGIONAL OFFICES

Canadian Council—800.560.8242, ccrj@urj.org

Great Lakes Council/Chicago Federation—800.650.8242, glc@urj.org
Regional Director of Department of Outreach and Membership
Julie Webb, jwebb@urj.org

Greater New York Council—888.634.8242, gnycrs@urj.org

Mid-Atlantic Council—888.842.8242, mac@urj.org
Regional Director of Department of Outreach and Membership
Ruth Goldberger, rgoldberger@urj.org

Midwest Council—888.692.8242, mwc@urj.org

New Jersey–West Hudson Valley Council—888.750.8242, njny@urj.org

Northeast Council—888.291.8242, nec@urj.org
Department of Outreach and Membership
Dr. Paula Brody, pbrody@urj.org

Northeast Lakes Council/Detroit Federation—888.282.6352, nelc@urj.org
Regional Director of Department of Outreach and Membership
Julie Webb, jwebb@urj.org

Pacific Central West Council—888.756.8242, pcw@urj.org
Director of Project Welcome for the Department of Outreach and Membership,
Karen Kushner, kkushner@urj.org

Pacific Northwest Council—888.294.8242, pnw@urj.org
Regional Director of Department of Outreach and Membership
Arlene Chernow, achernow@urj.org

Pacific Southwest Council—888.834.8242, psw@urj.org
Regional Director of Department of Outreach and Membership
Arlene Chernow, achernow@urj.org

Pennsylvania Council/Philadelphia Federation—800.368.1090, pac@urj.org
Regional Director of Department of Outreach and Membership
Ruth Goldberger, rgoldberger@urj.or

Southeast Council—888.289.8242, sec@urj.org

Southwest Council—888.234.8242, swc@urj.org

NOTES

NOTES